MW01137653

ONLY IN
SANTA FE

ONLY IN
SANTA FE

Denise Kusel

Sunstone
Press

SANTA FE

The opinions and ideas expressed in this book
are not necessarily those of the publisher.

On the Cover: Envelope Unopened by Carol Anthony
From the Artist's Collection—For my Friend Denise

Sunstone books may be purchased for educational, business, or sales promotional use.
For information please write: Special Markets Department, Sunstone Press,
P.O. Box 2321, Santa Fe, New Mexico 87504-2321.

Library of Congress Cataloging-in-Publication Data:

Kusel, Denise, 1943-
    Only in Santa Fe / by Denise Kusel.
        p. cm.
    ISBN 0-86534-446-9 (softcover)
    1. Santa Fe (N.M.)—Social life and customs—Anecdotes. 2. Santa Fe (N.M.)—
Biography—Anecdotes. 3. Kusel, Denise, 1943—Anecdotes. I. Title.

F804.S25K87 2004
978.9'56—dc22
                                2004019378

WWW.SUNSTONEPRESS.COM
SUNSTONE PRESS / POST OFFICE BOX 2321 / SANTA FE, NM 87504-2321 /USA
(505) 988-4418 / *ORDERS ONLY* (800) 243-5644 / FAX (505) 988-1025

To my parents who gave me a sense of humor.
To Leslie Rich for giving me the courage to use it.

One hundred percent of the author's profits from this book will go to the women and children of New Mexico to fight poverty and hunger through a fund administered by the New Mexico Women's Foundation.

A special thanks to *The New Mexican,* which graciously allowed me to use these columns that first appeared in the newspaper.

CONTENTS

3 GETTING ALONG / 83

4 LIVING IN SANTA FE / 129

INTRODUCTION

When I first moved to Santa Fe about 26 years ago, I cried. I didn't know anyone. Didn't have a job. All the houses were the same color. The streets didn't make any sense, often turning into one-way roads at whim.

Then something happened. I began to enjoy the idea that nothing made sense. Nothing worked. Nothing was expected to work, including the telephones when it rained. But no one really cared. Life went on.

When I wrote my first check for $2.56 for breakfast in a place most people spoke Spanglish and the chile was hot enough to spring tears into my eyes, I knew I had arrived in a place that mattered.

It was a place where people wore western hats, dusty boots and blue jeans. In the true tradition of the American West, people left you alone, unless you didn't want to be alone, and then they embraced you.

I discovered that I had to leave my native California to go East in order to get West. I won't say that living is easy here; it's not. But it's good.

The people are truly wonderful and for the past six years, I've been able to tell their stories, sometimes helping them find their own voices, sometimes using my own.

I learned a long time ago a good journalist writes the truth with love. Just as I've learned that I've never met a person who didn't have a story to tell. Here are some of those stories. Just the way they were when I wrote them.

—Denise Kusel
Santa Fe, New Mexico
2004

1

DOG TOWN DIFFERENT

It's All in the Eyes

This story really begins in the checkout line at Albertson's. It's packed with the kind of serendipity that we love here in Santa Fe. But for me, it began with a phone call from artist Sharon McConnell.

"You'll never believe this," she blurted into the receiver.

But knowing Sharon, no one with an ounce of logic would believe anything she was doing. She has a way of taking strange situations and making them even stranger.

"I was on my way to Whole Foods, but something told me to go to Albertson's in DeVargas instead," Sharon said. "Well, Bella and I were standing in the checkout line, and the man behind me said he has a dog that looks just like Bella. I told him that I got Bella from Guide Dogs for the Blind, up in San Rafael, Calif."

Now this is where the story gets strange.

"He told me that his dog was from Guide Dogs, too, but that the dog didn't finish his training," she said.

Bella actually did graduate from guide dog training, but sometimes you'd never know it. She's overly friendly and loves to give kisses, even to strangers.

But the important thing is she helps Sharon get around and manages to keep her out of trouble. Most of the time. Sharon is one of these lively people who seems to court strange experiences

"Then the man told me that his dog is named Count Bassie, and that he's five years old, which is the exact same age as Bella," Sharon said. "At Guide Dogs for the Blind, dogs receive their names in alphabetical order and according to what date they were born.

"I remembering thinking, `Wouldn't it be strange if Bella and Bassie were littermates?' So I asked him if he knew his dog's birthday. It was the exact same day as Bella's. I couldn't wait to get home to call Guide Dogs for the Blind to check to see if the dogs were related."

By this time in her story, Sharon was so excited, she was yelling into the phone.

"Well, they are; they're littermates! Can you believe it? Bella has a brother right here in Santa Fe. They could become friends and play together. But there's just one problem," she said. "I didn't get the guy's name or telephone number.

"You need to help find this man for me," Sharon shouted. "You need to write about it, so he'll call."

"I just can't write something like, 'If you have a dog named Count Bassie and you shop at Albertson's, please call me.' "Do it for Bella."
"I can't possibly do this, Sharon. I'm a professional journalist."

A Kiss Only a Mother Could Tell

Soliciting a phone call from a stranger with a Labrador retriever named Count Bassie resulted in some interesting replies.

First came a whispered news tip giving up the name and phone number of the dog's owner.

Next came a few emails from readers who said they knew the dog but not his owner, which is typical Santa Fe behavior, where we often know various dogs, but don't have a clue about their owners.

Here's a recap of the scenario: Sculptor Sharon McConnell and her guide dog Bella were in the checkout line at Albertson's. That's when they met Hank Bremer, who was waiting to check out. Hank told Sharon that he and his wife also had a dog from Guide Dogs, but that his dog,

Count Bassie, didn't finish the program, which in guide dog parlance is called "a career change."

"It was just the way Bella looked at me," Hank explained, adding that the dog looked exactly like his own dog.

But when Bella licked his hand exactly the same way that Count Bassie does, Hank knew the dogs were related.

"After observing Bella, I could tell both dogs had very much the same temperament," Hank said.

Count Bassie has lived with Teresa and Hank Bremer since they adopted him from the Guide Dogs for the Blind's career-change program.

"Only about 50 percent of the dogs in training graduate as guide dogs," said Guide Dogs spokesperson Morry Angell. "The majority of these dogs end up being returned to their puppy raisers to live as pets. For the small percentage of dogs that are available for adoption we go through a lengthy screening process."

When the Bremer's applied, they were one of 3,000 families on the adoption list.

"Before they consider you, Guide Dogs sends out someone from the local humane society to check your house, making sure the yard is fenced," Hank said. "They carefully check your references and history, finally matching the animal to you and your lifestyle."

If something untoward happens and Bassie could no longer live with the Bremer's, Guide Dogs for the Blind cheerfully will take the dog back, which is far more than most of our parents would do for us.

Additional information may be obtained by calling (800) 295-4050, and asking for a career change adoption application.

Guide Dogs also operates a newsy Website at www.guidedogs.com that contains such information as where the dogs come from, how they are raised and basic information about the program.

Bella and Count Bassie had their first play-date last Wednesday. Tails wagged; kisses flew. It was love at first sight.

Black & White & Speckled All Over

I've got this dog who's so sweet, everyone thinks he is a she. And that included the vet who had just given him his yearly exam and rabies vaccine.

"She's really a nice dog," the vet said.

"He," I replied. "He is a nice dog."

So nice, in fact, we decided to see if Callie could qualify as a therapy dog, visiting people in hospitals and nursing homes.

It hasn't always been easy for Callie. He's a 13-year-old mix of Border collie and Springer spaniel. When anyone asks, I say that he's a Santa Fe River Dog.

We're Callie's third home. He was adopted from the Santa Fe Animal Shelter & Humane Society by a young woman who after deciding she couldn't keep him, left him on our doorstep. That's how this sweet-hearted black and white speckled dog found his way into my life.

Callie, who weighs in about 40 lbs., rarely barks; waits his turn at the food bowl and sleeps on his assigned dog bed without complaint. However, he has one bad habit. He likes to sit on laps.

In fact, he once went running through a neighbor's open door, jumped up onto the lap of an unsuspecting woman and kissed her.

One day, to test his skills at sheep herding, I made an appointment and I took him out to Running Dog Ranch in Galisteo.

He walked into the livestock pen, and stood there looking at the sheep and wagging his tail. They took one look at him and walked away. Their tails were wagging, too.

"She's too nice," the herding instructor said.

"He," I corrected. "He's too nice."

Through the years, Callie's eyes have grown dim, and he's a little hard of hearing these days.

We almost lost him last fall after he developed diabetes. It took patience on both our parts to stabilize his blood sugar. He must now have two shots of insulin a day.

Sandi Miller, coordinator of the Animal Shelter's Pet Outreach Program, came over to see if Callie were suited for the program, which currently has 60 dogs enrolled.

She walked into the house with a checklist of requirements attached to her clipboard. No sooner had she sat down on the couch then Callie was right there leaning into her and calmly fixing her with those gentle eyes of his.

"She's friendly," Sandi said as Callie kissed her on the ear.

"He," I said. "Callie is a he."

Sandi nodded, made a notation on her checklist and endured another nose to the ear.

"I'm thinking about visits to children's diabetes support group," Sandy said. "How soon can she start?"

"Anytime," I said. "She can start anytime."

If you have sweet dog, Sandi Miller's number is 983-4838.

By the way, she's a push over for a kiss on the ear. Sandi, not Callie.

Loving Animals to Death

They work in the hardest part of darkness—the part found deep within their bizarre minds. They are called collectors, and for animals, they are the worst nightmare imaginable.

While the phenomenon of hoarding animals is not new, the psycho-sociological study of the people caught in this twisted web is just beginning to be understood.

Collectors share deep emotional attachments to the animals they are hoarding. These emotions, however, cloud the picture, laying a gentle fog over the judgment of right and wrong.

Animals are kept in cages, often in their own feces. They are routinely starved, stressed, mangy and ignored. This indeed is a strange love.

"There are probably many more collectors than any of us are aware of," said Kate Rindy, director of the Santa Fe Animal Shelter & Humane Society.

"These people usually lead very isolated lives, and turn to their animals as a source of love.

"We had a case earlier this summer here in Santa Fe. This person had 41 animals in her house. She lived alone, although she had relatives who lived nearby. She had a profession where she worked with animals on a regular basis."

After a long pause, Rindy continued to tell a story that has become strangely familiar to humane societies across the country.

"The pathology is always there. It's just that it doesn't get recognized. In this case, we were called in on a Sunday morning after the police found the woman dead inside her house."

Rindy removed her glasses and rubbed her eyes. "We found animals that had been kept in cages so long they no longer had muscle tone left in their bodies. Some of the cats had their eyes stuck shut. It was like walking into a nightmare. The hard part of the darkness is that people don't want to see what's happening and as a result animals are suffering."

As Rindy tells the story, it is her eyes that fill with passion and brim with tears, while her voice remains quiet. The result is disconcerting, like the calm before a storm.

"These cases are hard for me," she continued. "They go on day after day; night after night. My experience with collectors is that they leave town after being caught and take their pathology with them."

Rindy has worked for animal shelters and human societies for 20 years, the last five of them in Santa Fe.

Although the study of animal collectors is a relatively new one, researchers like Gary Patronek, VMD, PhD, of Tufts University, have built a profile of the typical animal hoarder.

o   Three-quarters of animal hoarders are women
o   Nearly half are 60 years or older
o   Almost three-quarters are single, divorced or widowed; more than half live alone
o   Cats are involved in 65 percent of the cases; dogs are next with 60 percent; followed by farm animals, 11 percent; and birds, 11 percent.
o   Hoarders have an average of 39 animals, with some having more than 100.
o   Reasons hoarders offered for their behavior include a love of animals; a view of the animals as surrogate children; feelings that no one else would care for the animals; and a fear that the animals would be euthanized if taken to a shelter.
o   In most cases, they live in unsanitary clutter
o   Prosecution is often long and difficult to resolve; even after removal of the animals, resumption of hoarding is common
o   There often is an inability or unwillingness of mental health, social service and public health agencies to get involved

Perhaps Santa Fe's most widely known case of animal collecting involved artist Tommy Macaione, a beloved oil painter who died in the early 1990s. Macaione was an eccentric animal lover who lived alone. He, himself, was cared for by various members of the community.

One of his caregivers tells this story:

"I used to get calls in the middle of the night from Tommy, crying to me that his animals were hungry and he needed to go out and buy them some food. We'd go to the store and buy bags of dog and cat food, and go over to one of his houses where he kept the animals.

"Tommy no longer lived in the house. There wasn't any room, so he lived down the street with another family that let him sleep on their sofa. When we got there, Tommy unlocked the door, and the smell from inside that house almost knocked me over.

"Tommy just emptied the dog food onto the floor. He kept the cats in cages with wooden floors. You know how cats bury their feces, well these had almost scratched through the wood. Some of them were just lying in the cages. I didn't know if they were alive or dead. I don't think Tommy knew either."

The man swallowed hard, and looked out of the window. He said the stench was so bad it had become trapped in his clothes. After he left, he burned them. He also called the police.

Tommy Macaione had two houses where he kept animals. The second, was out in Rowe.

Usually, the scenario is so horrific people are inured and often don't see it, or can't believe what is happening. As Gary Patronek pointed out in his research published in the January/February 1999 issue of "Public Health Reports," one of the key problems is that animal hoarding cases involve numerous agencies, yet often no single agency is willing or able to assume complete authority for the investigation.

Patronek said that because animal care and control agencies are obliged to address the animal care aspect of the problem, they are often left to struggle alone to resolve the entire case, though they may lack the authority and resources to do so.

"Four years ago in Cuba, N.M., we had a case of a collector who lived on a farm. He was a retired war veteran," Rindy said. "He had collected

160 animals. When we got there, we found 22 dead animals, while others were cannibalizing each other. It took us three years to get this case resolved."

The resolution? The man received a small fine and was limited to keeping only five dogs.

Unfortunately, animal hoarding is not widely recognized as symptomatic of a mental disorder, but instead is considered a lifestyle.

Adding to the difficulties is that animal collectors, Rindy said, are often charismatic people, often in profound denial that any problem even exists.

Once convicted of cruelty and sentenced to counseling, they are incapable or unwilling to stop collecting; that is, when anything is done at all.

"It's rare that cases are reported at all," Rindy said shaking her head. "These cases stand out as different than other cruelties. It's about stepping into the realm of the most horrible kind of darkness."

The frightening dynamic is these people don't recognize their own cruelty. They love animals. In fact, they love them to death.

Dog Town Different

While everyone in the world is receiving email spam promising to improve their sex lives through various enhancements, I regularly receive spam about septic tank improvements.

That's just how my life seems to go. Take dogs, for example. In my yard, I have four with wet noses and wagging tails; however, three act nothing like the books promised.

I was reminded of this at the 2003 Westmuttster, sponsored by the

Santa Fe Animal Shelter & Humane Society, where I was a judge, once again proving that some people will do anything for a free T-shirt.

Since this is Santa Fe, the Dog Town Different, I thought I'd share my vast knowledge of breed standards vs. reality and the types of canines with which a number of us share our lives.

The Basset Hound: The basset is known as a scent hound and can smell anything within a 50-mile radius, especially if it is sitting on top of a kitchen counter. Their two main pastimes are eating and sleeping. Bassets always sleep horizontally in a bed belonging to humans, thereby pinning you to the edge. Bassets also snore loudly, saving you the trouble.

Poodles: These dogs are noted for their intelligence and often are ready for college long before your children. When inviting a poodle into your home, you should immediately set up an educational fund.

Chihuahua: The Chihuahua should not be permitted around larger dogs since they will invariably beat them up, thereby inflicting the other animal with a massive lack of self-esteem.

Border Collies: Have a habit of staring and need to wear sunglasses since they have been known to hypnotize people into feeding them at odd moments. Borders need other animals around to chase; otherwise, they will begin herding you, your children and other neighborhood pets at every opportunity.

Santa Fe Curbsetter: These dogs are part Chow, Husky, Corgi, Australian Shepherd and Chihuahua. They usually have small legs and oblong bodies and are far smarter than the average poodle.

Often Curbsetters have one blue eye, one brown eye; one ear that stands upright while the other flops over; and a black spot somewhere on their tongues.

The Average Black Dog: There really are no completely black dogs in Santa Fe. They usually have a white spot somewhere and lots of freckles on their bellies. They are very good with children, but need their own beds since they must sleep with all of their toys.

The Reddish-Brown Dog: This dog is known for giving kisses and an uncanny ability to retrieve all objects, whether or not they belong to you. They especially enjoy going for rides, walks and staring at you until you take them somewhere.

If your dog's breed does not appear in this list, write to me to complain, since I know you will anyway.

The 6 a.m. Adventure

Block letters printed on the box proclaimed, "Needs no special tools! Assembles within minutes using a household screwdriver and a wrench."

That's a blatant lie gullible Americans everywhere continue to swallow even though we know better.

There's usually a happy family pictured on the outside of the box. They are using the very product you have just purchased. They're having fun. And then the biggest lie, they are still talking to each other.

I recently took home a similar box. Inside was the invisible, electric fence guaranteed to contain my wayward dog. After all, I'm a responsible pet owner. When the existing wall failed to keep him in, I erected barriers, beginning with wooden skids and odd lengths of chicken wire. Eat your heart out, Martha Stewart.

The dog sailed over the top almost as soon as I hammered in the last nail. That's when I decided on the electric fence. The going rate for having one installed is about $1,500. This includes someone coming over to your home, trenching the wire, hooking it up and then teaching the dog to stay away from the fence.

On the other hand, the cost of the DIY fence was $220, which is how I came to own a box that promised, "Installs in seconds. No tools needed!"

We decided to run the wire early one morning, before work, and before the heat of the day. First, we read the instructions aloud. I think it helps to hear the words as well as read them. Next, we got the requisite household tools.

"What's the screwdriver doing in the drawer with the wrenches?" I asked.

And that started it off. There we were, two people who can't remember nouns trying to work together and screaming at each other at 6:30 a.m. after promising each other at 6:28 a.m. we would be calm and mature.

Two hours and 45 minutes later, the wire was strung around the perimeter of the house. We didn't bother to trench because we don't have soil. Three days later, the little flags marking the boundaries were in place.

One week later, we got up enough courage to plug in the transformer and walk around the house holding the dog collar while we listened for the tell-tale beeping noise to assure us everything was working.

Two weeks later, the dog is still running around. Because although everything is working, no one wants to be the one to put the collar on the dog, just in case he should get a shock.

Next time, I'll tell you about the time I put the wheels on the BBQ on backward with my ordinary household tools.

Now Listen Up

It's always good to start off a New Year with new rules. It's a good time to level the playing field, which is why I posted a large note in the kitchen warning, "In 2003, there will be no dogs eating at the table."

I read it to Morley. He's a basset hound with a rather prodigious proboscis, which is a fancy way of saying big nose.

If you've never lived with a basset hound, they are quite unlike other dogs, beginning with low-rider legs right up to the prodigious proboscis, which can ferret out the tiniest morsel of food anywhere in the house.

I also showed it to Yoda the Corgi. I just held her up so she could read it for herself.

Yes, she reads. She also watches TV, is adept at simple math and can recognize a smallish dog cookie from a much larger one.

"No more dogs at the table," I reiterated. "I'm taking your chairs away right now."

This was met with a snort of silence. In truth, Yoda doesn't exactly sit at the table; she perches beneath it. In addition to her higher mathematical abilities, she's also a keen judge of character. She can tell the person most likely to drop food on the floor and situates herself accordingly.

Next comes Paddy. He's my woolly bully, a bearded collie with whom I share a similar hairstyle, sans the beard. Paddy's a shy guy and usually is content to sit beneath the portal on his own Taos couch with a hand-carved wooden frame.

Paddy is not a chowhound; however, he has thoroughly memorized the phrase, "Let's go get sheep." We go sheep herding together. Actually, I just drive the car; he does the herding.

Let's not forget Callie, a graduate of the Santa Fe Animal Shelter's cute puppy school. Callie is a quiet fellow. He's quite deaf, can hardly see, suffers from diabetes and needs insulin shots twice a day, but his nose still works and he knows where the kitchen table is located.

He sits next to the table in case you should suddenly fall out of your chair and your plate ends up on the floor. He's helpful that way.

Morley was the only one who really seemed distressed about the new rule. He began to sulk, walking out of the kitchen and into my office, where he has another chair that belongs to him.

He immediately languished into true basset behavior and fell asleep, snoring loudly and probably dreaming of better days when he had his own chairs in every room in the house.

To console him, I gave him a biscuit, which he took into the bedroom, jumped up on the bed and began eating on my pillow.

But rules are rules. He wasn't at the table.

Canus Barkus

I went to my first dog show last weekend. It was the major one of the year down at the State Fair Grounds in Albuquerque. Although I share my life with lots of animals, I'd never been to a dog show because it's not my type of thing. I didn't know what I was missing.

It was like seeing all those breeds we only look at in passing on the chart at the vet's office, all groomed to within one-inch of their lives. It was hard to believe that I had the same canus barkus ordinarius at home.

Sadly, competition was lacking in events open to the rest of us who found our mixed breed pets at the Animal Shelter, which is why I have included them here.

Dog with the Most Flatulence While Watching TV—Usually lies

innocently at your feet and appears to be sleeping, while making your life miserable.

Dog Most Likely to Shed—Stays outside until after you have cleaned house and vacuumed the rugs before deciding to come inside.

Most Food-Centered Dog—Usually found with its nose glued to the floor. Can be found waiting patiently beneath the kitchen table during mealtimes—yours, not theirs.

Dog Most Likely to Eat an Unguarded Bowl of Ice Cream—Using a rare form of ESP, which you and I as humans no longer have, the dog knows when you have left the room for more than 30 seconds and is able to down a pint of Cherry Garcia without leaving a lick.

Dog With the Greatest Ability to Counter Cruise—Although only a little taller than a standard Chihuahua, this dog has the ability to morph itself into a much larger animal in order to reach the tops of kitchen counters.

Santa Fe Curbsetter—Comes in all sizes, colors and hairstyles and displays selective hearing. In fact, the only way to recognize this breed is by performing this crucial experiment in the safety of your own kitchen.

First, call the dog, and wait 10 seconds. If it responds by immediately sitting at your feet, you do not have a Santa Fe Curbsetter, but rather a rare breed never before seen anywhere in the world. Next, call the dog again. If it ignores you, but thumps its tail on the floor, you have a mixed breed, probably from Taos. Finally, go into the next room, quickly closing the door behind you and turning the TV on loudly. Gently move the dog's food bowl across the floor no more than one inch. If the dog responds by throwing itself at the door, howling and begging to get in, you have a genuine Santa Fe Curbsetter.

Love Happens

Our story begins in a paddock in Cerrillos on one of these wonderful Northern New Mexico mornings. The sky is blue and there's a slight breeze.

Carried on the very tips of the wind is the whinny of a black mare named Chandel. Her feet paw the soft earth and she sniffs the air. She is searching for M&M, a Peruvian Paso Fino, and she is making these small nickering sounds because she is in love.

Springtime is a wonderful time to be in love, but neither Chandel nor M&M are exactly in the springtime of their lives. In fact, their story is about being old and blind and lame and getting a second chance.

But we all know that there's no accounting for when love happens. It just does. And for Chandel, a 33-year-old blind mare, it came wrapped in a package of a 25-year-old Paso gelding whose gait was long forgotten in lameness.

"She can't see him, but she senses he's nearby," said Suzanne Jackson, caretaker at the Horse Shelter where Chandel and M&M are living out their days. "She can smell him.

"They share a paddock, about an acre. They eat side by side. And when he's not right there, she neighs for him. He likes to be near her, and they stand next to one another," Jackson said. "Love is blind. This says it all."

Chandel was the first equine to call The Horse Shelter home. In two short years, the shelter has grown from providing a home for one horse to 15.

"We got a call about a month ago from down near Edgewood. This woman said her neighbors had moved away and left their horse behind," Jackson said. "Hard to believe, but people do this."

M&M is crippled and doesn't get around well. Jackson said when he first arrived, he was underweight and his eyes had sunk into his skull.

"Neighbors (in Edgewood) made sure he had water and some food, but he hadn't been groomed in months, and he had tufts of hair sticking out all over. He was sorry looking."

But then he met Chandel, who had retired a couple of years ago from an exemplary career with Challenge New Mexico, where she helped create dreams for kids and adults who had handicaps of their own.

M&M began eating. He embraced life with a new passion. And he fell in love with Chandel.

"They're inseparable," said Jackson, who has spent her life around horses.

With the average age for a horse at about 25 to 30 years, we owe these animals more than a one-way ticket to the killers. That's how Jan Bandler felt when she started the ranch on 130 acres and a dream.

But Chandel and M&M aren't the only love story out at the ranch. There may be one waiting for your family.

Taking a Bite Out of Obedience

Santa Fe is such a dog town that most of us believe we not only knew our dogs in a past life, but are related by birth or marriage.

Of course, I'm not an exception. In a past life I have been my dog's mother, and in another, his dancing partner. It's this last relationship that caused me to sign up for a Basic Manner's class. He was zigging while I was zagging.

In case you don't know, Basic Manners has replaced the old dog obedience classes. Let's fact it, we use so many euphemisms these days you can't always tell what people are talking about anyway.

Since so many of us have dogs, I'll bet more Santa Feans know the inside of that tan building on Agua Fria near Silar Road better than they know the inside of their local church. This is where the Santa Fe Dog Obedience Club holds its classes.

Most dogs enroll for more than one six-week class. Not because they're slow, it's because the person on the other end of the leash just doesn't get it the first time around.

The teacher of my class was Sherry Thommen. While the rest of us are working with pronged collars trying to coax our dogs to sit, all Sherry has to do is shoot the dogs a look and they immediately roll over, belly up trying to ingratiate themselves to her.

Now I don't want to say that Sherry is overly strict, but the other day she walked into a gallery opening and half the people dropped to a sit-stay position, while the other half began watching her instead of the art. The two who didn't were tourists who were considering moving here.

The other morning I walked into class and Ro Hofberg, the owner of a Basenji named Dulcie waved me over.

"Dulcie, sit," Ro said smugly. The dog sat. Ro smiled, pulling a sandwich baggie from her pocket to reward her dog with a hotdog treat.

I reached into my pocket and pulled out my own baggie of sliced hotdogs.

"Paddy, sit," I said to my bearded collie after shoving a hotdog in front of his nose. He looked at me as if he had never heard his name before and didn't know who I was. He turned his head in another direction.

"What are you feeding him?" Ro barked.

"Jenny-O turkey dogs," I replied.

"Dulcie only eats Hebrew National," Ro sniffed.

The room grew unnaturally silent. Sherry had walked in.
"How many of you did the homework?" she asked.

"I did," I said, waving my hand wildly. Lying about homework is not new for me. I had plenty of practice in college. It sort of comes natural.

Sherry gave me a hard look. People have been known to confess to crimes they'd only read about happening in far away cities when Sherry fixes them with an eye. I sat down quietly and began panting.

"I don't think you practiced," she said.

"How can you say that?" I whimpered, my voice climbing six octaves.

"I know you," she snapped.

Just then, I understood it all. I had known Sherry in a past life. But don't even bother wondering who was top dog.

The Sad Saga of Raisin

The saga of Raisin the cat begins at the State Pen. It seems there are a number of cats around the prison south of Santa Fe because the inmates feed them.

Raisin was one of the cats that hung around the yard, existing on scraps of food tossed out by guys just a little hungry for something soft in their lives.

On some days, Raisin would sit in the sun and groom herself the way cats do, first using one paw and then the other. The light made her sable-colored fur shine.

But for some reason known only to a few cruel and inhuman men wearing uniforms, Raisin's life took a turn for the worst.

It seems two prison guards got a little bored one day and began booting Raisin around. There's no need to go into the details, just keep in mind who the culprits were and who the victim was.

Raisin was eventually rescued, whisked from the prison under the noses of the grumbling guards who implied threats of retribution if the cat were removed from the prison.

The cat was brought to the Santa Fe Animal Shelter & Humane Society by a petite woman, who asked her name not be used because she works out at the prison and is afraid for her life.

The veterinarian reported that the guards had driven a metal ring through Raisin's tail and had kicked her in the eye. In addition, the vet said that there were a series of tiny pin-pricks all over her underside as if someone had stuck thumb tacks into her tiny stomach.

Through perseverance and prayers, Raisin eventually was nursed back to health at the shelter and eventually adopted out.

It took six months for Raisin to recuperate from the trauma and massive infection. It took less than six minutes for two people to see Raisin and fall in love with her goodness.

"The other day, Raisin's new owners, Geoff and Tina, stopped by the animal shelter," said Kay Lockridge, who volunteers at the facility. "They came in to finish some paperwork on a kitten they had adopted for Raisin at the pet adoption clinic the shelter runs at Pet Smart last week.

"Apparently, Raisin had become friends with a neighbor cat and, when he goes home (the other cat is allowed outside; but Raisin isn't), Raisin seemed to miss him. So, Geoff and Tina got Raisin her very own little kitten, which she grooms, plays with and protects."

While this is a happy ending to what might have easily been a horror story, we need to remember that not all animals walk on all fours.

A Passel of Pooches

It's time for one of Santa Fe's premier social events—the Westmuttster Dog Show, when a passel of pooches get to strut their stuff in front of a crowd of admirers.

Despite being pummeled by allegations of bribery and bad judgment, I have once again been asked to serve as a judge. Period. So there.

To be truthful, I didn't exactly jump at the chance. I had wanted to enter Paddy in the owner-dog look-alike contest. But not even someone as blatant as I could enter and judge at the same time. So, I put my own hopes of recognition and fame on the back burner for the good of the community.

It was not an easy decision. But during a weak moment, I happen to answer the phone.

"Hello, this is Denise."

"Hi, this is Kate Rindy, director of the Animal Shelter & Humane Society. How are you today?"

"Not well," I sniffed. "My life has gone to the dogs."

"That's a compliment where I work," she barked. "I want to ask you something."

"I won't do it," I yelped.

"Won't do what?"

"Be a judge at the Westmuttster. I have plans of entering one of the contests myself," I whined.

"By yourself?" she snorted. "Just report to the quad at the College of Santa Fe for registration from 11:30 a.m. to 12:30 on Sunday. The contest starts at 12:30."

"No! Didn't you hear me?" I howled.

"No one says no to me," she nipped.

She's right. Kate has this reputation of always getting her way, sort of like a cheeky Chihuahua out on a Saturday night binge.

"OK, tell me about the events," I wailed.

"You already know about the owner-dog look-alike contest. There's also best trick. Best use of a wagging tail. Best costume. Best old-timer. Best all-around dog. And did I mention the look-alike?"

"Yes, a couple of times. Paddy and I coulda been contendas," I drooled. "Even my mother says we look alike."

"Paddy isn't even an Animal Shelter alumnus," Kate bayed. "He couldn't have entered anyway. The Westmuttster is only open to dogs from shelters—any shelter. And this time bring your own snacks. That incident with the dog biscuits last year was absolutely embarrassing."

"I was hungry," I panted. "I thought you guys were going to supply lunch."

I paused to lick my wounds but I didn't cry. Honest. The last time I cried into the telephone, I shorted out both the receiver and the answering machine.

"Look, Denise, I'll even give you a Shelter T-shirt that says, `Cold nose, warm heart,' and it has a picture on it."

"My picture?"

"Yeah, there's a certain resemblance," she yipped.

When Customer Service Goes to the Dogs

"This phone call may be monitored for training purposes," the auspicious voice announced.

Of course, they never tell you what kind of training. Besides, in order to speak to a real voice, it takes a lot of fancy finger work on the telephone keypad.

But after Morley, my basset hound, received his very own, pre-approved Platinum Diamond fixed-rate credit card complete with a chance to have his photograph on the card, I began playing the numbers game.

Don't even concern yourself with the fact that while I'm paying 18 percent on my credit card, he'll be paying 2.9 percent to the same company.

So I picked up the phone. After I was warned that all the credit information imparted would be available to a bevy of interested people, I was asked for Morley's mother's maiden name.

"How come?" I asked.

"Because of the Patriot Act," the voice warned.

That's when I let the cat out of the bag. "Morley is my dog," I nipped.

"Are you telling me you have applied for a credit card in your dog's name?" came the reply.

"No," I answered. "I didn't apply. He was pre-approved."

"What is his Social Security number?" she hissed.

"That's silly," I said. "He hasn't worked a day in his life."

"He's unemployed and he's trying to get one of our Platinum Diamond Preferred cards?"

"You offered it to him through the mail," I barked.

"I don't know how he got into our data base if he's unemployed," she said thoughtfully.

"Well, he did apply for Worker's Comp once after he got sick eating a four-lb. bag of Hershey's Kisses."

"The kind with the nuts?" she asked.

"No," I answered. "The originals in the silver foil wrappers."

"I think you'll have to call the Social Security Administration to have his credit reinstated. Just press two."

"Press two? You mean you're also Social Security?"

"We're in the credit business, honey. We get you coming and going."

I pressed two, and waited.

"How can I help you?" a voice asked.

"Wait a minute. I just spoke to you. This is the same voice!"

"Of course this is same voice," she said. "I'm the same person. It's part of our downsizing in an effort to save the consumer money. I'm really the only human being working here."

"But you didn't help me before," I complained.

"That's right," she chortled. "And don't count on me helping you now, either. Did you press two?"

"Yeah, I did, but I got you again."

"Try pressing eight," she suggested.

"What's on eight?"

"Me."

"Well, who's on seven?"

"No, Who's on six."

"But what's on one?"

"I already told you, What's on eight."

"I thought you were on eight?"

"That was before. I got a promotion."

"For what?"

"For customer service, that's what."

2

EVERYDAY PEOPLE

She Passed this Way Once

When Death hangs around your door, you placate him with ritual. A stuffed toy here, a doll there. Plastic flowers. Real flowers. A tiny wooden cross with a small space for a name.

And if there's money enough, a headstone to identify who is resting there.

For Amy Jobe, there was no money. There was only Marker 24, Spot 15 at Rosario Cemetery. Today, while other mothers are taking their daughters shopping for clothing, Linda Jobe is looking for something special, something to leave a mark, something to remind that her daughter passed this way once.

"We try to put something there," Linda said. "We've had small dolls. Flowers. Little pictures. As soon as we put something down, it's missing the next day. I guess someone needs it more than we do."

On December 6, 1999, her daughter was riding her purple ten-speed on the side of the road on US 84/285, when she was struck and killed by a passing motorist.

"I knew the moment it happened," Linda said. "The dog started howling. He was devoted to her. After Amy died, he wouldn't eat for days. We had to put one of her slippers in his crate."

Linda has spread newspaper clippings on the table in front of her. They are limp from being read so many times.

Amy was special from the day she was born. Linda said the umbilical cord was wrapped around her daughter's tiny neck, depriving her of oxygen. By the time she was four, she had stopped developing mentally. And later, although she looked like a young woman, she would stay a small child the remainder of her life.

"I still talk to her," Linda said. Her fingers moved quietly, folding and refolding the newspaper clippings. "I dream about her all the time. It's been a tough two years. It's a mother's nightmare, walking out and seeing your daughter's shoe at the end of the driveway."

Amy was a student at Pojoaque High School. When she died, students who had known of the young girl's love for animals brought stuffed toys to the funeral. Linda still keeps them on a special shelf as a reminder.

"I gave away her clothes," Linda said. "But I can't give these (toys) away. I'm not ready yet."

At the side of the kitchen table, Patches, the small black and white mixed breed dog, was taking an afternoon nap. Occasionally, he'd open an eye to check that all was well.

"Amy was my gift from God," Linda said. "I learned so much about love from her. She was my little hummingbird."

Amy Jobe's birthday is tomorrow. She would have been 18.

Things Mattered to Her

Everyone called her Arlene. She didn't need a last name. But before she died Friday night after a massive stroke, the name Arlene LewAllen had become synonymous with art in Santa Fe.

Arlene was different things to different people, and whatever she was, she was genuine.

Things mattered to her. People mattered. Art mattered. Kindness mattered. She had a habit of taking your hand in both of hers to pull you into whatever she was doing at the time. She let you know you counted, and along the way, made us feel as if what we were doing also counted.

She approached life with a breathless sincerity; there was always so much she wanted you to see. Little escaped her, certainly nothing in our art world did.

Friday night openings either began or ended at Arlene's because that's where we went to discuss the work we had seen. No matter what you knew about art, or thought you knew about it, she made you feel safe to talk about it.

She was here working at Hill's Gallery when it helped redefine Santa Fe art. And, later, when she opened her own gallery, she brought us there with her. Hung us on the walls. Gave us a chance to make money from art and raise our families here in a town we loved.

She was here in the early 1970s, when Santa Fe began touting itself as a place that mattered in art. She was here to watch us grow into the dream. Arlene was one of us—an old hippie who made good.

As news of her death began filtering through the community, it was accompanied by a collective sadness. There was such an outpouring of emotion because that's the way she lived her life, with emotion.

She treated artists with dignity, taking time to look at our portfolios when other galleries wouldn't even let us in the door. As one painter said, "she was right at the same level as the artist." She never thought she was more important because she was the head honcho. To her, the art and the person making it were both important.

She also took the time for a journalist who knew less about art than the proverbial person who knows what he likes. I always knew if I had a question, I could ask Arlene. Just as I knew the answer I received would be the truth.

And now there are tears because we're so sad. I think she'd tell us it's OK to cry, but I think she'd also remind us not to dwell on it. There's just too much to be done.

A Farewell to Bill Lumpkins

It was standing room only at the St. Francis Auditorium. In fact, they had to open the balcony. I saw people I hadn't seen in years Tuesday when more than 500 Santa Feans turned out to bid goodbye to their friend William Lumpkins.

The people in the auditorium represented a cross-section of the city: Hispanic, African American, Native American, Anglo. There was gray hair, spiked hair, a baby with no hair, and a couple of high-crowned western hats.

Bill would have liked it because on some level everyone he met was important to him. And that's the way he treated them, with dignity and respect no matter who they were or what they did.

That's just the kind of guy Bill was: A simple man of quality. At 90, he had lived a varied and rich life, witnessing nearly a century of technological and social changes so radical that it boggles to think about it.

When he died on March 20, he was known as an architect who pioneered passive solar design and a painter, but more importantly, to a number of us, he was neighbor and a friend. He once said he needed both the discipline of architecture and the freedom of painting. The two formed a good balance.

For me, Bill encompassed what it meant to be a Santa Fean. He loved this quirky town, and from the looks of the people at his memorial, it loved him as well. You might just say, both were well suited to each other; each with a wry grin and a sense of humor about life in a place no one can really change.

I first knew him as an artist, an abstract painter and someone who cut a dashing figure at art openings wearing Levis, sports jacket, a pair of boots, a dapper ascot scarf around his neck and a trademark flat-brimmed Stetson.

It was only after I had interviewed him a few times and got to know him that I came to have an understanding of how much more he really was.

He was born in a simple ranch house near Clayton, N.M., on a spread with the unlikely name of Rabbit Ears. And while he spent his early years in a part of the state that isn't usually known for liberal attitudes, somewhere along the way he developed them on his own. They must have made an indelible impression on him because they stuck.

He fought the good fight all of his life, mounting a forceful campaign against injustice by bringing this town its first chapter of the American Civil Liberties Union and later a branch of the Legal Aid Society.

Still later, he spearheaded a family health clinic for those who otherwise couldn't afford health care.

The last time I sat down and talked with Bill, life had slowed down for him. But when he spoke about fighting against injustice, his eyes bristled with energy and then softened with hope.

His attitude about the way we deal with our brothers and sisters remained positive, and I greatly admired him for it.

At the memorial, one by one people stood to share their "Bill stories" mentioning such things as the fact that he lived to witness a dream come true in the formation of an educational arts center, the Santa Fe Art Institute.

But it was Viola Montoya, a longtime friend of the family, who said what was in our hearts, "Sweet dreams, handsome cowboy."

A Sea Cruise Along Route 66

When Bozo Cordova was a kid, people would stop by the gas station where he worked in Santa Rosa to fill up their water bags before continuing on Route 66. Gas was 20 cents a gallon.

"I dragged raced on 66. We'd go out there, park, drink cold beer. I've done it all here on this highway."

Today, he's doing something else on this particular bend of Historic Route 66. He's opened the Route 66 Auto Museum (www.route66 automuseum.com), which is where I met him. On this particular morning, we're sitting at a chrome and vinyl dinette set in the front room of the museum. Wilbur Harrison is singing "Sea Cruise" on an oldie soundtrack loop.

Route 66 memorabilia is festooned throughout the room, along with child-size paddle cars and trucks taking me right back to a kid scene of my own.

Bozo has spent his life in Santa Rosa, with the highway broadcasting his every dream, from hanging with his friends at the Del Rey Café to rooting for the Santa Rosa High School Lions.

And then there are the cars.

"Back then, you could tell a Mercury from a Chevy," Bozo says. His eyes are glistening with memories of all those superfine cars with their bulging hunks of chrome, hard plastic steering wheels, broad fenders and fins, and push-button radios set to KOMA 1520 out of Oklahoma City.

That was the radio station that played the hits. And if you were a kid and cruising Route 66 in the Fifties, that's what you listened to.

"C'mon, I want to show you something," Bozo tells me.

We duck into another room, the other half of this massive warehouse building. This is where he keeps his dream machines. The cream puffs with their mirror gloss paint and tuck and roll upholstery.

"I rebuild these to my specs," Bozo brags. "I drive a '47 Chevy convertible built on a 1987 Corvette rolling chassis."

Some of the cars have their hoods up, and I look inside and nod. These are the cars of my youth. I know about the engines. They were from a time when you could open the hood and see what was wrong.

"Back then, all you needed was a set of points, a vacuum check and a volt meter," Bozo smiles. "Look at this 1956 Chevy four-door convertible. Looks like a truck, right? But Chevy didn't intro the El Camino until '59. That's why I have this one, 'One of None'."

A '39 Chevy, two-door sedan with a chopped top and doors with shaved handles stands nearby a couch fashioned from the backseat of a '57 Chevy convertible with those unmistakable fins jutting out, and the seat is a cool tuck and roll. Bozo says he'll build me one for $5,000.

Bozo is cool. He's got this smile that doesn't quit. He's got his cars. And just out the front door, he's got his highway.

What Does Brahms Have in Common With Chubby Checker?

The thought of spending the summer just a few feet away from the principal cellist for the Santa Fe Opera wasn't exactly music to my ears.

The opera had rented him a casita on the property where I live, and prior to his arrival I had nightmares of meeting in the driveway and having nothing to say to each other.

What did we have in common? He'd be talking Brahms. I'd be talking Chubby Checker. He'd be talking Handel. I'd be talking Hendrix.

What if he'd ask me a question about opera? After all, I was arts editor for this newspaper for about 15 years. I'm expected to know something about classical music.

All the "what ifs" in the world melted away when I first laid eyes on Bryan Epperson, the principal cellist for the Canadian Opera Company, a faculty member of the Glenn Gould Professional School of the Royal Conservatory of Music in Toronto, a founding member of the Cambridge Chamber Music Society and the string trio Triskelion.

Even his hands are insured for something like three million.

His whole being exuded a large appetite for life. His hair stuck out in 12 directions. He looked like a mad man. His eyes danced with a passion about life. His neatly trimmed beard and mustache embraced a mischievous smile.

He was beguiling. He introduced me to a new wine. I showed him the fine points of tequila. He showed me his 248-year-old cello. I showed him my concertina with the wooden button that Gerry Carthy made for me when the original one fell off. He played Mozart. I played "Danny Boy."

He had just come from a week's horse trek in Wyoming. Jazz was drifting out of the car radio. I was in love. I ran in to email my mother. He said he was married. I decided to email anyway. Soon he was drinking tequila, and I was sipping wine.

That was the summer of '99, when I learned more about opera in two months than I had in 25 years of listening to the Texaco's Metropolitan Opera radio broadcasts.

Bryan Epperson returned this summer. I am no less smitten. He and his wife, Charlotte, a producer with the Canadian Broadcasting Company, have become part of our family.

I can't imagine summer without Bryan. In the late afternoons, I sit out in the driveway between our two houses and listen to him practice.

After he returns from a night at the opera, he likes to sit beneath the portal and smoke a cigar while listening to the coyotes.

Bryan loves Santa Fe. He said he dreams about it when he's back in Toronto, especially on those endless winter nights.

He is a good student. He's learned about Gran Gold margaritas at Maria's; impossibly magnificent sunsets; and summer mornings so beautiful you have to blink your eyes to make sure it's real.

On Monday nights he has volunteered to take the trashcan down to the road. He hefts it aloft, carrying it with those hands that are insured for more money than most of us will ever see in our lives.

Last Sunday, I introduced him to a time-honored Santa Fe tradition. I took him to Jackalope.

Each summer, both the Chamber Music Festival and The Santa Fe Opera enrich our lives, and you don't have to know the difference between Handel and Hendrix to find the right notes.

Chuey Breaks the Mold

A couple of years ago, no one would have thought Father's Day would mean something to Jesus "Chuey" Gonzales, least of all him.

The men in Chuey's family led lives colored by alcohol and violence. His father was a drunk and walked out when Chuey was a baby; his uncles made decisions with their fists.

Father's Day was the last thing on his mind in 1995 at the New Mexico Boys School in Springer, where at 18 he was doing time for armed robbery.

Meanwhile, in Santa Fe, his girlfriend was strung out on crack cocaine and about to give birth to their baby. Within four years, Chuey would have two children by two different mothers

Today, at 23, Chuey has spent a good chunk of his life behind bars, and considering his life's history, he might have stayed there. But he got a chance to change his life. He was given an opportunity to show what kind of stuff he was really made of. Oddly enough, it was fatherhood that provided the wakeup call.

About five months ago, a social worker he had met while in Springer called and told him about the New Mexico Young Fathers Project.

That phone call gave Chuey a chance to rewrite the next chapter of his life by getting involved in a program that helped him learn male nurturing and the role of fathers in the lives of their children. It turned his life around.

Chuey's story is one of struggle. The struggle to get sober and off drugs. The struggle to get free of a gang. The struggle to take control of his life. The struggle to understand what it means to be a father and a husband.

It's been a real uphill battle, and it hasn't been easy. In fact, Chuey's life has been anything but easy. Most of the males in his family have a history of violence, drinking and jail. They were his role models.

Before he was 20, he knew what it was like to be on the run. Staying power was never one his habits. When he'd had it with life at Springer, he walked.

"I just got tired of being locked up," Chuey said simply.

After a few months of drinking and partying, he found himself back in Springer, which was where he was when he found out he was a father.

"She was born when I was in there," Chuey said of his daughter, Santana. "Her mom was doing crack. She was with another guy. My mother brought (Santana) to see me when she was just a few weeks old."

Within the year, Chuey was back on the streets and released to the Reintegration Center, a halfway program for juvenile offenders in Albuquerque.

"I had started working," he said. "But then my daughter got real sick and began having seizures. She ended up in the hospital in Albuquerque.

Social Services got involved and ended up releasing my little girl back to her mother."

Chuey speaks quietly. When he mentions his daughter, his eyes grow intense with concern. It doesn't take long to see that he has a real affinity for children.

"After the hospital, her mother took her back to Santa Fe and then they disappeared. No one could find them. I ran from the center. I had to find them, and I did. My little girl wasn't being cared for. She wasn't even wearing diapers when I found her. I took her with me, back to my mother's house. Less than a month later, my baby's mother showed up with the cops."

Chuey was sent back in the halfway program in Albuquerque. After he was paroled in 1998, the first thing he did was get drunk.

"I just had all this stuff coming at me," he said. "I couldn't handle it. The responsibility of being alone; of being a father. I lost the chance to get my little girl back."

Somewhere along the way, Chuey got tired of running. Maybe it was the war veterans he met while doing community service. Maybe it was meeting the woman he eventually married.

"I got into this relationship, and my girlfriend got pregnant. I said to myself, `Oh, not again.' That's when we got into parenting classes at La Familia," he said.

He attended classes with his girlfriend, who had a son from a prior relationship. It was here that Chuey learned about discipline without violence.

"That was a big one," he said. "It was hard for me not to be violent. My step-dad was violent. My uncles were violent. I didn't meet my own father until I was 12, when my mother dropped me off at his house because I was always in trouble. On my 13th birthday, my father came home drunk and told me to get out. I thought all of life was like this. Drinking. Violence."

Some of these memories fueled his desire to take parenting classes.

"I told myself this can't be happening any more. My dad wasn't there for me. This has to stop somewhere. I have to be there for my children."

At this point in his life, Chuey was living beneath a camper-shell. In the mornings, he'd catch a bus to the Community College where he was taking classes. His girlfriend and her son were living with her grandparents. After a few months, so was Chuey.

When their son Luis was born, Chuey and his girlfriend were married.

He found himself the father of two, but with few tools to handle life's problems. He began sliding back into old ways, dealing with his problems through the neck of a bottle.

That's when the phone rang. It was Cissy Ludlow, a counselor with Catholic Social Services, who was calling to tell him about a new program, the New Mexico Young Fathers Project.

The project is basically funded by the New Mexico Department of Health and Human Services. Its goal is to work with young fathers, helping them learn about nurturing and how to be a cogent member of the parenting team.

The program gave Chuey a survival tool. It taught him there was more to life than just himself.

"I thought to myself, before you walk away, just think of what you went through and what it would do to your child if you walked away," he said.

Today, Chuey is mentoring other young fathers, helping them find the elusive answers about what it means to be a parent and how to do things as a family.

"It's precious to have a family, he said. "Growing up, it was all I ever wanted. I'm grateful. It's a gift from God."

An Afternoon With Drew

Drew Metheny gave me a long look before he decided to share his popcorn. After he had made the decision, a disarming smile spread across his young face as he extended the bowl toward me.

This sharing meant more than it appears. Drew, who is 17, was born with a condition called Prader-Willi Syndrome, so sharing his food was a big deal.

One of the symptoms of this relatively rare condition is an insatiable appetite traced to a malfunction of the hypothalamus, the part of the brain that controls hunger and satiety. After Drew has eaten, he still feels hungry, and it's a feeling that cannot be controlled, even with appetite suppressants.

Throughout the day, Drew's mother, Susan Metheny carefully metes out her son's caloric intake, which is limited to 1,500 calories per day. This means he eats 15 separate meals a day, with about 100 calories per meal.

That's a lot of work, but after spending some time with Drew, it's easy to see how it's all worth it.

He is what my Hispanic neighbors call a true *innocente*, someone who will always remain innocent in the eyes of God.

One of the causes of Prader-Willi has been traced to missing information located on Chromosome 15. Varying degrees of mental retardation and learning disabilities also are part of the picture.

"During my pregnancy, I knew something was wrong, but the doctors kept telling me everything was fine," Susan said. "Drew was born on Valentine's Day in 1983. My whole life changed that year."

Nature can be cruel. Drew's condition is compounded because he also suffered complications at birth and is confined to a wheelchair. Along with the manifestations of his condition, deep within him, Drew seems to know what's going on, although he cannot fully articulate it.

In addition to attending various meetings on the rights of the handicapped, Susan spends all day, every day seeing to his needs.

Respite care just isn't in the cards. Drew's name is on what's known as the "waiver list." He is waiting for his number to be called so that his mom can get a little help taking care of him.

In New Mexico, for every $26 dollars allocated by the State Legislature, the federally administered Medicaid program pays four dollars as a participation match. In order to modify the regular Medicaid rules, a state must ask the feds for a waiver.

Under this waiver, eligible individuals may receive specialized services in their home as an alternative to living in an institution. Drew is one of 2,000 people on the waiver list.

Last year, 464 found their way off. This year, only 200 managed to get off. It is, vocational rehabilitation officials say, a matter of legislative appropriations: Names come off the waiver list as funds are made available.

Drew's name has been on the waiver list since 1998; other individuals have had their names there for more than five years.

In the meantime, Drew Metheny waits.

And waits.

Susan sees it as an issue of individuals being denied their civil rights. Civil rights can be legislated; but there is no legislating compassion.

"Have I been bitter? Was my life over as I knew it? Absolutely. But would I go back to the person I was, no I would not. Drew has definitely expanded my consciousness," Susan said softly.

"Sometimes, when people meet Drew, they cry. They see him as less of a person, but he's not. He just has different needs. He's given me an opportunity to learn so much. I can't imagine my life without him."

In searching for the resources to help him, Susan inadvertently has become an advocate for the handicapped. It's not something she planned, but it's something at which she excels.

She now helps other parents throughout the country dig their way through the muck and mire of the medical bureaucracy to find answers to help make their lives bearable.

"I'm used to being brushed off (by the health services establishment)," Susan said. "Others are brushed off, too. Somehow, it makes it all easier to bear. But it doesn't make it nice."

There's a photograph of Drew on the piano. He's hugging Santa Claus, only his smile is far bigger and more genuine than the one Santa is wearing. I couldn't help but think who was giving and who was receiving.

Following our visit, I signed on to a Prader-Willi Web site on the Internet to find additional information. The messages on the online bulletin board were succinct. More than one read, "Please, somebody help me."

A Tale of Fabian and Lola

Fabian Duranona's paintings are not easy. They have as many layers as the man himself, perhaps more, perhaps less. It's hard to tell.

Each holds a labyrinth of secrets, hidden until you are ready for them. Images are tucked into images, and are seldom what they seem at first.

Fabian was born in Argentina. His father escaped the country when friends of the family began to disappear. He feared he was next.

"We were one of the *decamisadoes*—the shirtless ones," Fabian said in an accent that is curiously Queens and Argentinean. New York is where the family landed when Fabian's father sent for them in 1976.

For a young boy who ran from the horrors of a dictatorship, he found solace in his paintings and in the dream of owning a dog one day.

Fabian arrived here about 10 years ago, holding down odd restaurant jobs, getting by and living for the hours he could stand in front of a canvas wielding a paintbrush and allowing his thoughts to stream out. Like squeezing a tube of paint, he wanted to wring the most from life.

"I was walking by the church (Santuario de Guadalupe) one night after work and I heard this loud voice. It said, `You can have a dog now.' The next day, I found Lola," he said.

Understand that before this he was totally alone. But something shifted for Fabian that night.

Sometimes a dog can give us a reason for being. They help us see things; teach us how to take the time to experience life's velvet moments. That's the way it is for Fabian and Lola.

Fabian, whose birthday is on Christmas Day, lives in a small house behind another house at 609 1/2 Agua Fria. He says he welcomes people to stop by and see his art.

Inside there is one chair and a stove. A record player and a stack of LPs share a small table. In one corner, Lola's blankets are neatly folded.

At night, Fabian will unroll his own pallet on the floor near Lola and beneath his paintings that cover every wall.

He's between jobs right now, so when I stopped by to see him, he was able to spend some time with me, taking me on a tour of his psyche.

"When I paint, I'm invisible. I don't know if I am spiritually more advanced or if I have a vitamin deficiency," he joked.

The canvases burst with color. They are at once frightening and inviting. They are the stuff of sweet dreams and nightmares.

And of course, Lola is in every painting, only you may have to look hard to find her.

A Breath of Air With Gerry

The biggest problem with talking to Gerry Carthy after he returns home from a trip to Ireland is that you can't understand a word he's saying. If his accent were any thicker, we'd have to meet in a pub.

As it was we were sitting at his kitchen table here in Santa Fe and he had just pulled out a coffee can stuffed with screwdrivers and an assortment of dental files.

Gerry was taking apart my concertina because the "air" button that controls the bellows had sneaked beneath the metal faceplate and was playing hard to get.

Without "getting air" as it's called, the notes wheeze like someone allergic to chamisa on a sunny Santa Fe day in the fall.

My concertina was made in Italy. The good ones are made in England, Ireland and Germany. I like to think that my particular concertina once belonged to a Gypsy who traveled in a wagon with no one but a monkey for company.

Gerry is a street musician, which is a bit of a romantic notion in itself. His uniform includes a couple of shirts layered for warmth and a tweed cap with a shock of curly hair sticking out every which way. A beard covers most of his face, and his eyes harbor an amused twinkle. He says he likes playing on the streets because it fits with how he approaches his music.

"Street music is part of my Irish tradition," Gerry said.
But not in Santa Fe, where it is against the law to play music on the streets. To even approach the Plaza carrying an instrument is suspect. We seem to have the idea that only drifters play on the streets.

"It makes no difference if I'm playing at the Hotel Loretto or out on the street, it's all about the music," Gerry said, jumping up to unplug the teakettle. He dumped a handful of tea into the pot and gave it a quick stir.

"This is Irish tea. Brought it back myself," he said pouring me a mug. He splashed some milk into my cup and did the same for himself before going back to working on the squeezebox.

"What people don't understand is that when I'm playing a hymn like `Amazing Grace,' I'm praying."

Prayer in any form plays a big part in Gerry's life. It helped give him the strength to get off the bottle.

He's been in the United States for 16 years, one more year than he's been in Santa Fe. I first met him outside of Alfalfa's, where he was playing penny whistle and concertina.

Someone had given me a concertina and I asked Gerry to give me lessons.

Every week, I'd sit at the kitchen table and squeak out Gaelic songs with words I couldn't pronounce. But Gerry could. He'd chide me for insisting on playing with a sheet of music in front of me. He doesn't need written notes. It's something he feels deep within him.

"I have a relationship with the music, not with the page," he said.

Gerry is on the Artists-in-Residence program through New Mexico Arts, which means that the state recognizes Gerry and his traditional Irish music as a cultural asset, but the City of Santa Fe won't let him play it on the streets.

A Larger Than Life Guy

Jack Loeffler is one of these larger than life guys who moves through his place in time with truth and honesty.

It hasn't made him wealthy, but it's made him immensely rich in other ways.

"I've never had more than just enough," he told me once.

Jack's got a new book out, a memoir of his antics with his friend Ed Abbey,

Adventures with Ed: a portrait of Abbey, UNM Press.

Abbey was an environmental activist and the author of such books as "Desert Solitaire" and "The Monkey Wrench Gang."

But I didn't go to see Jack about Abbey, I went to his house, which is a shake beyond El Dorado, because, quite truthfully, like a lot of us these days, I was hungry for some real and honest talk.

Jack sports a Hemingway beard and has taken to jotting notes in the kind of moleskin notebook used by Hemingway and Bruce Chatwin. Like both of these writers, Jack is a raconteur, a natural storyteller who draws nourishment from adventure.

"What I am is a refugee from a B. Travel novel," he said, punctuating the thought with a laugh.

Jack likes to joke that he's been "gainfully unemployed for all of his life," but the truth is he's involved in important work, collecting the stories, songs and folklore that help reflect the rich cultural brew of the intermountain Southwest.

"I figure I put on about 30,000 miles a year using my trusty Subaru in the winter and my pickup during the summer months," he said.

"I'm getting ready to go back to Chenille (Canyon de Chelly), where I've been working with some Navajo kids, teaching them how to record their songs and stories. It's a project I'm doing with photographer Bruce Hucko called `Voices of Youth."

Jack has two offices in Santa Fe, both stuffed with tapes, both reel-to-reel and DAT, a historic testament to his work as an ethnomusicologist.

These days he's is mulling over the hypothesis of *querencia*, a place where you get your energy.

"It's a safe place where you find your own reckoning, your home country," Jack said. "I feel at home all over the Southwest, any place west of the 100th meridian."

It really doesn't matter where you were born, but where you call home. It's a sense of place, somewhere you go to recharge your batteries.

"I literally turned on my first tape recorder in 1964 at Navajo Mountain in Utah where I lived in a forked-stick hogan for seven months," Jack said.

"I began to recognize that understanding the bond between culture and habitat is our only chance. My real work is wandering around and understanding cultures and helping them record their history."

Betwixt and between his travels, Jack is working on his autobiography, "A Life Without Tenure."

Makes sense, doesn't it.

Making Sense of History

It takes time to make sense out of history. We need to provide enough breathing room to give it the respect it needs so we can understand what it is that happened.

For a lot of us, this is how we're finally able to deal with Vietnam, an aspect of our collective history as Americans that we are just getting the distance to confront.

It will always be a war that burns questions on our lips and brings tears to our eyes, but a lot of healing has the chance to happen.

For Jane Carson, that time is now. When Carson was a 24-year-old nurse fresh out of school, she found herself in Chu Lei, Vietnam. It was in 1969-70 during the height of the war buildup.

"I not only lost a lot of friends, but I can still see those young men who came in blown to bits," Carson said. "They were barely old enough to shave, and there we were trying to put them back together and send them back to the States.

"We didn't have time to grieve. We never even debriefed or talked about the serious things. I volunteered to go to Vietnam thinking I knew what I was going to face; but I hadn't a clue. I wasn't prepared. None of us were. We were all afraid, but all not wanting to talk about it. Instead we just stuffed it all down."

Now Carson, who is retired from a 27-year military career, is ready to face the ghosts. She's ready to go back to Vietnam.

"I've never been back to Vietnam," she said. "I wasn't ready. I didn't even go to the Wall (the Vietnam Veterans Memorial) until 1989. I started working with Diane Evans on the Vietnam Women's Memorial and through that process I was able to talk with other women."

That was when I first met Jane Carson. In 1993, she accompanied the Vietnam Women's Memorial on a whistle stop tour of the United States on its way to its final resting place on the National Mall, just yards from Maya Lin's Wall.

To help interpret a forgotten part of the war, the Vietnam Women's Memorial committee hired Santa Fe sculptor Glenna Goodacre.

Goodacre sculpted a heroic-size bronze depicting three Vietnam-era women caring for a wounded soldier, and then joined the memorial as it rolled through the countryside from Santa Fe to Washington D.C. on the back of a flatbed Fed-Ex truck.

The monument touched everyone who came in contact with it. The truck was driven by a Vietnam vet who after two days on the road wore the haunted look of a soldier on a never-ending night mission, which played across his face in the headlights of oncoming cars.

I went along to write stories for The New Mexican, stopping with the monument at prearranged locations to interview people along the way.

I can still see the face of a man dressed in fatigues in a wheelchair who pushed himself up to the statue just as the sun was setting in Bryant Park in New York City.

He placed his Purple Heart medal in the hands of one of the nurses depicted in bronze and rolled silently away. The scars of this war were still raw and slow in healing.

"The 'Nam vets, no one could possibly understand what we had been through," said Carson, who relocated to Santa Fe in 1997. "The greeting we got when we got back. We were told not to wear our uniforms. I was this young nurse who proudly went off to Vietnam, and (when I returned) found it hard to understand why my Army green uniform was the target of cruel jokes and sometimes outright hostility."

The names of eight military women and one civilian who died in service to their country will be remembered in the building of a series of health clinics made possible through a Christian group called VietAid, which has been supplying medical equipment and medicine to Vietnam.

Additional information on VietAid may be obtained online at Lanson@casagrande.com.

"The medical care for people in Vietnam is almost non-existent," Carson said. "One of the clinics we're going to build is in Chu Lai, where I was stationed about 320 miles northeast of Saigon on the South China Sea."

Since Carson has lived in Santa Fe, she has become active in community service and animal rights.

But it's when she talks about the horrors of the war that her South Carolina accent grows thick and quiet, as if she were mumbling to herself, still witnessing the carnage and waste of human life.

Her mission today is one of forgiveness and healing—to remember, forgive and let go—so that the fullness of life can march on.

"I was afraid that my heart would break if I ever allowed all of my emotions and feelings to surface, but as Alice Walker wrote, sometimes 'breaking the heart, opens it.'"

The greeting that Vietnam vets often share with one another is one that the country forgot, "Welcome home."

Welcome home, Jane.

Trying to Put the Puzzles Together

Long before Hannibal Lecter gnawed his way into our consciousness in "Silence of the Lambs." Long before Jeffrey Dahmer got the urge to digest his conquests, there were others.

"And there will be again," warned forensic psychologist Mick Jepsen, a soft-spoken guy with an accent that immediately gives away his southern roots.

As gentle as Jepsen seems, it was horror of cannibalism that sparked his interest leading to a career in forensic psychology. His motive was simple:

"I was just trying to put together the puzzle of why people would do that sort of thing."

He recounted the story of a young man in his mid-20s who lived a quiet life with his father until something went terribly wrong.

"He murdered his father, cut him up and put him in the freezer," Jepsen said. "Over time, he began cooking and eating him. The neighbors began complaining about a bad odor."

I sought out Jepsen because I've been haunted by the stories of the Santa Fe cat mutilations, which some are dismissing as a teenage prank. But calling it a prank cheapens the crime, dismissing it as a rite of passage.

Jepsen, who is licensed to practice forensic psychology in three states including New Mexico, has spent more than 25 years studying kids who kill.

He has become an expert in why individuals did what they did, what led to a specific crime and why they chose a particular behavior.

"With kids and young people in particular, you can see a bunch of red flags that signal high risk for violence and harmful aggression toward others. You see this particular with animal abuse," he said.

"One of the interesting things is that people who are psychotic or mentally ill and commit sexual homicides and sexual aggressive kinds of things often are abusive to animals, and to cats in particular."

Jepsen speculated that cats are abused because they are not as responsive to humans as dogs.

"We're talking about control issues, and because a lot of homicides are about power and control issues," Jepsen said.

He pointed out that adolescence is a prime time for antisocial kinds of behavior.

"Most chronic antisocial behavior that lasts into adulthood began before adolescence," he said. "Aggression is a learned behavior, a way of coping with deficit social skills. If you see harmful aggression in pre-adolescent kids that involves injuring or killing animals or other kids, especially when they have no appreciation of the impact of their behavior, than those kids are headed for trouble.

"Kids imitate a lot of what they see in moves without realizing the true impact," Jepsen said. "There's an inability to tell play from reality."

Does violence on TV fuel this behavior?

"There's no question," he said.

It's a Matter of Respect and Love

Claude's Bar was situated on a rutted dirt track called Canyon Road. Poet Witter Bynner held lively readings in his living room over on Buena Vista Street. *Death Comes for the Archbishop* was on the boards at The Santa Fe Community Theater.

The year was 1959, and Joe Paull and Bob Jerkins decided to try out life together.

Now 43 years later, Canyon Road no longer resembles a cozy meandering neighborhood byway. Witter Bynner's home is now a B&B.

The Community Theater has changed its name to Santa Fe Playhouse. But Joe and Bob are still together.

In fact, the two just held a Celebration of the Covenant at the United Church of Santa Fe.

"It was very humbling as the minister to have just turned 49 years old and to be standing in front of a couple who has been together for 43 years," said The Rev. Talitha Arnold.

Still others joked about "rushing into things" or suggested waiting until "they knew each other better."

When asked their key to success as a couple, "We compromise. We do everything Joe wants," Bob said quickly.

"It's a matter of respecting each other's interests," Joe said.

Right from the get go, Bob and Joe immersed themselves into the community.

For Bob, that meant community theater, appearing in more than 40 productions throughout the years.

"Back then, we were always looking for a place to hold the Fiesta Melodrama," Bob recalled. "Dorothy and Tom Donnelly found the property at 125 E. DeVargas. It was $35,000, and we were terrified because it was so much; but, we bought it anyway."

A few years ago, the theater paid off its mortgage and owns the prime piece of downtown real estate free and clear.

Meanwhile, for Joe, who earned a doctorate in social work, community involvement took the guise of civil rights activism.

"He (Joe) was responsible for the study that started a class action law suit by the ACLU leading to a decree reforming the laws for foster care in New Mexico," Bob said proudly.

The talk soon turned to Santa Fe characters.

"Oh, there was Winnie Beasley from Tesuque, who played the gut bucket and drove a motor cycle with a side car that had breasts," Bob said.

"Don't forget Scoopy Williams, the six-foot-one concert pianist," Joe added wistfully.

The two may have lived through one of the most exciting times in Santa Fe's recent social history, but they're still active in community affairs.

Bob is appearing in the Seniors Reaching Out benefit, "Mardi Gras November" on November 3rd at the Armory for the Arts.

However, on this morning the sun was shining into their living room as they planned their commitment ceremony, each sitting in his favorite chair, and each completing each other's sentences.

Some Generational Differences

Okay, so he's 19, and I'm a little older. That doesn't mean I can't be in a state of awe. I'm talking about Jonas Skardis, my computer guy.

True, there are some generational differences. He's talking virtual memory and I'm trying desperately to hold onto my own. He logs onto an underground Santa Fe web site to find out where the latest rave is, and I sign onto www.santafenewmexican.com to read the obits every morning to make sure I'm still alive.

He has his own Web site, and I'm still reading "Charlotte's Web."

But these differences are nothing. Basically, we're in love with the same computer—the Mac. The big difference is that Jonas knows how it works and I don't, which is how I met him in the first place.

Among other clients, Jonas handles the computers at SITE Santa Fe, which is used to doing business on the edge of the known world.

He also does troubleshooting for a friend who has a computer in every room in different colors to suit her moods.

"You should call Jonas," she said, after I explained my computer woes over a breakfast burrito at Tia Sophias. "He's a computer genius."

"Is he old enough to drive or do I have to pick him up?" I asked. After all, since I've been working at home and have to supply my own computer support, I've learned that anyone working in computers who is over the age of 13 doesn't know what they're doing.

"He has his own car," she said, quickly ordering another orange juice since it was my turn to pay for breakfast.

So, I bit the virtual bullet and gave Jonas a call. What I mean is I used my cell phone to call his cell phone and left a message.

Jonas was in New York attending Mac World, which is where they introduce all the new Mac goodies for the year. In a few nanoseconds, he returned my call.

"How come you didn't go to the Mac World in San Francisco? It's closer to Santa Fe?" I said trying to appear knowledgeable.

"I did," he answered.

We made arrangements to meet so I could guide him to my house, which in true Santa Fe style is located on a real street, but there are no street signs so it's hard to give directions.

The difference between us was apparent at once. He was driving a black Saab 6000. I was in a 1974 black and yellow Citroen Deu Chaveux, which clocks 0-to-60 in one day.

He walked into my office, looked at the cat and multiple dogs and flicked an imaginary piece of cat hair from his black anorak. I was glad I remembered to take the lunch dishes off my desk before he arrived.

Jonas has fit his entire life in a soft briefcase with compartments for his CDs, cell phone and PowerBook.

Within 15 minutes he had my computer up and running and had defragmented my hard drive, which sounds like something I wouldn't want to tell my mother about.

He told me about a couple of cool Web sites; we talked about the good old days when all computers were gray, and I was about to ask how he felt about older women when the alarm sounded on his Palm Pilot.

We made an appointment for the following week, which is about how long it would take me to crash my computer a million times and need help again.

In the meantime, we could always email.

Burro Alley Needs Chairs

I have a lot of respect for City Councilor Karen Heldmeyer. She's bright. Articulate. Honest. Concerned. Keeps in contact with her constituents.

But her recent vote against allowing tables and chairs on Burro Alley was a surprise and does a disservice to Santa Feans wanting to use Burro Alley as a viable and people friendly place.

She complained that "the more you fill it up, the less it is an ancient passageway."

Well, Karen, that's exactly right. By definition it remains an ancient passageway, but by today's standards Burro Alley also serves as a much-needed respite area in a downtown badly in need of such spaces.

Forget the burros and wood-sellers, Karen, they're not coming back. Maybe we should have thought about this before continuing to allow traffic to choke our downtown historic area.

Although I wish that the public might freely use the tables and chairs in Burro Alley whether or not we buy a glass of wine or a cup of coffee, as a realist I have long accepted that nearly everything we do downtown has a dollar sign in front of it.

Other councilors commented on Burro Alley:

Councilor Patti Bushee complained about the bollards at either end. The answer is a no-brainer, Patti. Turn the bollards into planters so we actually can have living plants in the area.

Councilor David Pfeffer was quoted as hoping that other cafes seek to put tables and chairs on public rights of way.

Great idea, David. Why don't you shepherd the way through the mire of red tape that prevents other restaurants from doing just that? But remember to make it affordable for the small business people as well as the larger ones.

"I'd love to see downtown filled with chairs and seats," he said. "I'd love to see liveliness everywhere."

A fine idea, David. Why don't we start with the area in front of the Palace of the Governor's?

Not only could we could have tables and chairs, but what about colorful shade-cloth stretched across that venerable byway? People would be grateful for the shade.

If you want to see downtown lively and vibrant, take the first step. After all, that's why you were elected—to make Santa Fe a better place for all citizens.

Councilman David Coss said the rents weren't high enough.

"I wonder if Gerald Peters would let you set up 18 tables for three months for $300?" he asked.

Tsk, tsk, David. Remember what Flower told Thumper: If you can't say anything nice, don't say anything at all.

We need havens like Burro Alley and the Plaza to point the way toward community. I loved the way the Pancake Breakfast infused the Plaza with activity and friendliness.

Too bad it lasted only a matter of hours.

We need action downtown. Not historical excuses.

When Mice Get the Better of You

You know how the phone rings importantly when it's someone with an urgent message? That's what happened Monday afternoon. It was Candelora Versace calling to tell me about her mouse problem.

"I've never seen so many mice," she squeaked. "They're doing a jig right outside on the patio, even as we speak."

She paused for a breath and I immediately jumped on the opportunity to say something. "Well."

"That's easy for you to say," she interrupted. "You don't live out here in the wilds of Eldorado."

"The wilds of Eldorado? Am I missing something?" I asked.

"We have this little pergola outside the back door. We put little Christmas lights around it so it looks pretty at night. It doesn't look like a dance hall or anything, just tiny, little white lights.

"Well, the other morning, you know what I found?" she asked rhetorically not really expecting an answer and certainly not giving me a chance to offer one. "The plug was eaten clean off. It was gone. All that was left were these little teeth marks on the electrical cord.

"And if that's not enough, the mice have now burrowed into my flowerpots. They eat the roots right off the plant.

"The other morning I went outside, stealing like a thief in the night with my little bucket of shower water to water my plants, we can't water out here, and all the flowers had all fallen over. There weren't any roots to hold them up."

"Have you tried one of those Have-a-Heart mouse traps?" I asked, watching a mouse scurrying into a small bush in my own yard. The problem with Xericscape is that you can always see through it no matter how many years ago you planted it.

"Have-a-Heart? Gimme a break," her voice dropped down to a whisper. "We tried De-Con. It was terrible having to use poison. I mean, I grew up in the '60s. I'm a politically evolved person. I'm a mother."

"Did it work?" I asked, adding De-Con to my own shopping list.

"No, it didn't work. We put it out at night and the next morning the whole damn box was gone. These mice are amazing. Did you know they walk up the stucco right along with the lizards?

"Then they got into the vent for the bathroom exhaust fan. We had to get a shop vac and blow them out. As if that wasn't enough, the dishwasher stopped working. The repairman removed the front panel where the sound insulation is. It was missing. The mice had taken the insulation for their nest."

"What about your husband?" I asked.

"No, he's still here. They haven't gotten him yet. Same with the cats. You know how we like to think cats have psychic abilities and are sitting around watching angels on the ceiling? They're really not. They're listening to the mice. I have to move back to the city."

"You mean New York?"

"No, Santa Fe. Remember that New York humorist Fran Leibowitz? She said, `Nature is what you walk through on your way from the apartment to the taxi cab.' Well, I agree. Tell me, do you have a mouse problem?"

"No," I lied.

Mommy Dearest is on Her Way

My mother is coming to visit me. You know what that means? I have to dust. I usually put in 20-watt bulbs, but now, with Daylight Savings Time, she's sure to notice. Besides she's had one of those laser surgeries and doesn't even need to wear glasses anymore.

Then there are all these dogs around here. I'll have to disguise them as something else. She doesn't like dogs.

"If it eats, I don't want to live with it," she told me.

Curiously that doesn't affect my father. After all these years, they are still married. I have come to believe that it's either true love or inertia. You remember inertia. It's how most people feel about their jobs. They don't exactly like them, but it's too much trouble to change.

I decided to call my mother to ask what her secret was for having a long marriage.

"Hey, Ma, it's me."

"Can't you call me Mother like a normal person? Can't you just say Mother, not Ma? Or Mommie Dearest. You may call me Mommie Dearest. Now hurry up and tell me what do you want, it's almost time for my show."

"I thought you'd be glad I called. Remember, you sent me that phone card from Sam's good for 500 minutes."

"You'd think at your age I wouldn't have to send you a phone card," my mother said. "Your brother calls me all the time."

"Ma, he never even left home."

"Very funny. He did leave home. He's coming over tonight for dinner. You were always jealous of him, your brother."

I didn't want to go there, so I changed the subject.

"Look, I want some advice. You and Dad have been married for a long time, what's your secret?"

"Who?"

"Dad. You and Dad have been married for more than 50 years, how have you managed to stay together that long?"

"We don't live together."

"C'mon, Ma, you do live together."

"Oh, is that who that man is?"

She paused for a moment. I could hear her drumming her fingers. You see, my mother always wanted a Girl Scout. Someone who would grow up and be Harriet Nelson. Instead, she ended up with someone who channels Harriet Nelson.

"The secret to a happy marriage is two TV sets," she said. "That way there's no arguing about what to watch. Now, I have to go, it's time for my show."

"What show is that, Ma?"

"My show. The one I watch," she said.

I should have remembered my mother was never one for giving up secrets.

Nick Ault: Private Eye

I picked up the phone to call Nick Ault's place. You see, Nick is a private eye. And me? I've been in enough gin joints and cheap diners to know which way is up.

So I punched in his cell phone. Nick doesn't have an office. He works out of his car.

"Nick baby, you don't know me. I mean really know me," I said in a breathy voice. "But I want to go out with you. You know, like on a stakeout."

"A steak-out?" he mumbled. "You mean that steak place up near Taos?"

I could tell he was playing hard to get. But I wasn't born yesterday.

"Very funny, Nick. I like a guy with a sense of humor."

I paused to remove the toothpick from the side of my mouth. It was making me lisp. I wanted to show him that I could be easy, only not too easy. Flexible, perhaps. "OK, well, what about the Sonic?"

Nick Ault grew up here in The Big Different. He's been a PI for more years than I could count. Maybe like 10. He wasn't always a PI, he used to be a city cop. He knows where the bodies are buried. We arranged to meet at Sonic.

When I drove up, I saw him sitting in his late-model Chevy with tinted windows. There were dice hanging from the rearview mirror. Nick's a lanky guy with a pair of pale green eyes you wouldn't dare lie to. There's a dark side to Nick, but I didn't want to know about it.

I parked my car and climbed into his. I ordered the usual. Two green chile cheeseburgers with onions. Two large orders of fries. Two drinks, with straws. A hot fudge sundae, two chocolate malts. A slice of pie. And a side of mustard.

I don't notice what he ordered. I figured he was a big boy, he could take care of himself.

But it didn't take us long to realize that we were being served by an amateur. Or maybe it was someone who just wanted to make it look like an amateur. There were ketchup and onions all over the take-out tray. I asked him if he knew of anyone who would want to hurt him.

"I know lots of people in this town, Denise," he said, checking the rear view mirror.

"Hey, how do you know my name?" I asked, pulling out a chocolate cigar from the inside pocket of my thrift store jacket.

"What do you mean, how do I know your name? Remember, it was you who called to set this up."

He had a point there. I didn't want to argue with him. Not just now. "Call me Velma," I said. "That's what all the dames are called in those film noir Dick Powell movies."

"Velma?"

"That's right, Slick, and smile when you say it."

"Dames? Hey, isn't that getting a little P.I?" he said.

"Is that PI as in Private Eye?" I asked out of the side of my mouth.

"No, that's P.I. as in Politically Incorrect," he said.

He was too fast for me. I began thinking of excuses about why I had to go home.

But things got easier after he put the car in gear and we rolled. You don't drive on a stakeout. You roll. I know these things.

The house was located in a suspicious neighborhood. Something about it looked faintly familiar. I noted the house was painted one of the 15 shades of brown accepted the Santa Fe historical group.

Even from the car, I could tell the adobe was fake. Up on the roof, a string of plastic bagolitos flapped in the breeze. One bulb was out.

Everything else looked good, only you'd need a compass to find your way from the front door to the mailbox.

There was something familiar about the neighborhood, but I just couldn't put my finger on it.

I slumped in my seat and looked over at Nick out of the corner of my eye. We'd been sitting there for five minutes and nothing had happened yet.

"Look here, Nick, let's dispense with the polite drinking, shall we?" I said, taking the last swallow from a can of Diet Dr. Pepper.

"Why don't you try to get some shut-eye. I think I'll go and put some powder on my nose," I said opening the car door.

"In the arroyo?" he said, stifling a yawn.

"Well, I misplaced my house key."

"Maybe it's time to head for home," he said.

Home? That's it. That's why the house looked familiar. It was my own house. I tried to act cool.

"You mean it's time to call it quits?" I gulped. "We haven't even seen any criminals yet. It's only 8:45 p.m."

He looked at me sheepishly. Then I knew. These may be the mean streets of The Big Different, but in Santa Fe everyone is home in bed by nine.

Turn Left at the Hot Water Heaters

There we were, sitting tall in the saddle. The air was sweet from our recent rains, which stained the sandy-bottomed arroyos a rich red.

To the east, the Sangre de Cristos were sprinkled white with snow. To the west, the Jemez were bathed in clouds. The whole world was the kind of quiet you can only find on horseback. My ponder and I could have been the only two people in the world.

"We'll be heading off to the right by those two water heaters," my companion said.

Water heaters? Wait a minute. What happened to this idyll? And sure enough, there they were. Two tin bodies, lying on their sides, reflecting the sun like discarded dreams.

"That's what happens when you charge people to haul things to the dump. They haul them out to the arroyos."

We rode along without talking for another few minutes. Discarded glass bottles gleamed like diamonds in the sun. Dented cans added to the local color.

Only now the early morning ride took on another dimension. I had to carefully guide my horse through some mounds of trash, I fixed my eyes on the horizon.

I was riding with writer William A. Luckey, author of a handful of westerns.

The thing that really distinguishes these books is they have more horses than people in them. Plus, there's this certain softness to them. The hero isn't always handsome. The women in the books aren't always drop-dead beautiful.

"So, do I call you Luckey?" I asked tentatively.

"Call me Belinda," the writer said. "William A. Luckey is just a nom de plume."

But that's where the make believe stops. Like her heroes, Belinda

Perry has spent most of her life in the saddle, but unlike the characters that people the pages, a good chunk of Belinda's life has been spent teaching people not to be afraid of horses.

"It just worked out that way," she said. "Most of my students are in mid-life and are realizing a dream of riding. I can read people pretty well. I know when they're scared about riding."

As soon as she said that, I realized I was holding onto the saddle horn. I gave the horse an awkward pat on the neck.

I hadn't been riding since I had spinal surgery two years ago. So, good to her word, Belinda and I weren't charging along, we were poking through what appeared to be the detritus of Santa Fe life.

"Do people usually talk a lot while riding?" I asked.

"Do they ever," Belinda said. "We talk about everything. It's good therapy. There's something about being on horseback that gives you the freedom to talk about anything, but especially about life."

I looked over at Belinda, and I just had to smile. Here was a woman who carved out her piece of life with a typewriter and a saddle.

She was wearing English riding jodhpurs, a western-style jacket, a pair of Aussie boots. She was on a horse that was outfitted with an English saddle and a western headstall. None of it mattered. No phoniness here.

She was happy. She knew who she was. And, podner, she looked great.

By the time we headed back to the stable, I had let go of the saddle horn and life was good. I even remembered to turn right at the hot water heaters.

Wally and Abigail

Abigail Ryan is a woman of decisions. Not that she actually follows them once she's made them. She doesn't.

When she came to Santa Fe to visit family, the plan was to just spend a week looking around town. That was seven years ago. She's still here.

When a friend gave her a dog that had been rescued from a ditch, she agreed to keep it overnight. That was three years ago. She still has him.

In fact, Wally the dog has changed her life, the way dogs often do. Life is a little more planned these days. Abigail hung up her backpack, quashing the habit of jumping on a plane and traveling at whim.

Besides whim may be a difficult habit to feed in these days of terrorist jitters.

So Abigail found herself in a new place and no job. But she had already been introduced to that Santa Fe tradition that says the best things in life are discovered through word-of-mouth.

She heard about a job available at a top-end furniture and home accessories store that needed someone to work in their furniture-finishing studio.

This was perfect for a woman like Abigail with a richly active imagination and a special knack for creating the kind of dream anyone could jump into at anytime.

"I worked at the studio for six years," Abigail said. "Then a client asked if I could create a wall finish that would continue the look of the furniture."

She could, and did. In fact she began creating entire rooms: Faux kitchens that carried the illusion of being in Tuscany. Cement floors waxed with a certain patina, producing the fantasy of walking on ancient surfaces.

"I do all sorts of faux walls and floors," Abigail said. She also dispelled a myth that it takes huge amounts of dinero to feed the imagination. "There are ways of doing things. Sometimes I leave out a few layers; other times, I just let my imagination run wild."

The subject of imagination and how artists invoke it is a fascinating one. I asked if she ever just closed her eyes and slipped inside the world she was creating.

"That's when time lets go," Abigail said. "It often depends on the job. I once did a sky (on the ceiling of) a wine cellar. I was painting and all of a sudden I'm in that world.

"The same thing happens when I'm working on a chair or a piece of furniture," she continued. "I have pictures or samples of paints used during a certain time period. In my mind, I can picture that chair in a room 200 years ago."

Her furniture and walls carry the look of time that has been waxed and dreamed away.

For a more distressed look, there is always Wally the dog.

Building a Home, One Roof at a Time

Most of us consider ourselves lucky to have a roof over our heads.

Katrin Smithback had seven. But the only luck involved was that they all didn't come crashing down at once.

It started small as most roof problems do, with a leak. Water the color of red dirt came smearing down an inside wall in the living room.

About 10 years ago Smithback invested in a new roof, so she figured it was time. Besides, it's usually the case when something happens, something else is sure to follow.

Smithback had just paid off a new septic system, so it stood to reason something else was bound to go wrong.

It did in April, which just happened to be the only amount of measurable rain this year.

Like most savvy Santa Feans, Smithback had long ago noted the name of a roofer and kept it just in case.

Enter Fred Vigil and his two sons who help him in the family business.

Also make note of the fact that for a lot of older homes built in Santa Fe County the rules about electricity, plumbing and building in general took a back seat to creativity.

Working diligently to fix the roof before the next rain, Vigil pulled off the old roof. And then pulled off another. And yet another, until he had removed equivalent to about 37 tons of stuff.

"I think I heard the house sigh when they removed all the old roofs," Smithback said.

The vigas sighed, too. Smithback estimated they "grew," leaving a two-inch gap where the walls touched the ceiling.

It's not uncommon for roofers to uncover one or two old roofs when they're doing new work. But seven? El gato was out of the bag. Someone got lazy.

According to Fred Ellis, whose artist-father Fremont Ellis owned about 400 acres at Rancho de Sebastian, Smithback's house was built in 1937, when a lot of the work was done by barter by guys who were just passing through. They'd work for a day or two and move along.

As if the story of the many roofs weren't enough, along came the trickling silt. The original roof really wasn't a roof at all. It was a bunch of dirt piled onto the latillas.

When most of it was removed, the rest filtered down onto the floor until there was a pile of 65-year-old silt eight inches deep on Smithback's living room floor.

There really is no end to this story. After constructing a superstructure on which to build a roof, the project is nearly finished.

But if you have a few minutes, I'd like to tell you about the old septic system. Turns out it was just a bunch of wooden boxes that had been bolted together.

At least the house isn't haunted.

Being Different is a Good Thing

Long ago in Santa Fe the Rubber Lady would show up on the Plaza, just to remind us that it was a good thing to be different.

She would silently sit wrapped in a form-fitting black rubber suit on a bench near Woolworth's, her immobile face masked in white rubber.

Other times, she might be in the bar at the old La Posada, quietly observing life, a silent community conscience.

I thought of her the other day when I saw a sign posted on the front door to the bank, "Please remove your hat and sunglasses." Like you, I am quite aware these days of the loss of our freedoms and civil rights.

I couldn't help but think that couched within the Rubber Lady's serenity was her unspoken right to diversity.

To get a perspective on New Year's Day 2003, I called that bastion of freethinking, the Rubber Lady.

Actually, no one really "calls" the Rubber Lady. She isn't listed in the phone book. Instead, I relied on a Santa Fe tradition: I asked around until she called me.

"Why don't I see you anymore?" I asked.

"Oh, I'm still around," she sighed. "You just have to look harder to find me.

"Times are different now and I can't be as open as I was back in

Rubber Lady's heyday of making appearances, when I was asking people to question and look deeply within themselves.

"In 1978, when Rubber Lady first made her appearance, the climate was one of curiosity. It drew people in, made them want to know more about their environment by understanding how all things are connected."

By the early 1990s, Rubber Lady said, life had drastically changed. People weren't as playful.

She began appearing less, until there only was the rare appearance when she might be seen talking to a child on the Plaza in her own silent way, while the child quietly examined this odd being wrapped in something resembling a big tire tube and a wet suit.

"Often times when a child looked fearfully at the Rubber Lady, the Rubber Lady would mirror that fear until it wasn't a fear anymore.

"But as the 1980s passed, Santa Fe grew away from small town life, rich with flourishing ideas and creativity, into someplace that had lost its innocence," she said. "Today, we run from the fears that are pervasive in our society."

One time it was enough that the Rubber Lady could just do ordinary things, but differently. She represented actions motivated by an innocence missing today.

"We need to ask deeper and greater questions remembering the anecdote to fear is wisdom," she said.

"When wisdom prevails over fear, the Rubber Lady will be back. When peace returns, look for me on the Plaza. I'll be there."

3

GETTING ALONG

A Faded Lady

Night wraps over Havana in a dark velvet, mysterious and plush.

The streets are oddly dark, broken up only by blue light pooling out of living rooms from occasional black and white TV or the ever-present florescent bulbs. Castro's Cuba may be wired for electricity, but that doesn't mean the utility gets delivered.

I am looking for a certain house, and a story that began in a Santa Fe restaurant with a promise to deliver a suitcase packed with soap, razor blades, shampoo, chocolate, T-shirts, note paper and other items culled to make daily life a little easier for an elderly woman.

But nothing's easy in Cuba, and I'm told that once in Havana, if I feel that I am being followed to simply put the suitcase down and walk away.

Along with the suitcase, I am handed an envelope with a letter and some money. The letter is sealed and is none of my business. In fact, aside from checking the contents of the suitcase, I don't ask questions. It's better that way, I am told. Safer. Because even in these strange days of semi thaw between Cuba and the United States nothing is certain.

Things can change at a moment's notice. I am warned life can be made difficult, and sometimes impossible, for someone with certain ties to relatives in the U.S.

But on this night, my first on this lush island, I am walking past the pastel colonial buildings I've seen in photographs. With the large Moorish arches, they are tawdry icons of yesterday's Havana. There are no shadows, no streetlights, but there is a slight moon and I begin checking out the lay of the land. If I don't know to whom I'm delivering the package, I want to at least understand where.

The neighborhood is an old one. It faces the sea. When there are breezes, they are balmy and delicious. In front of one house, a boy plays with a small dog enmeshed in the happiness of young boys and puppies everywhere. His mother sits on a crumbling stoop and watches him.

From inside the house, the ubiquitous blue light illuminates a room in restless flickers. Assorted chairs form a semicircle around the television that wears a crown of rabbit ears. On the surface, I could be home in northern New Mexico, with the small TV and the scattering of chairs, but here the dark is nearly absolute.

I literally cannot see in front of me and am resigned to walking down the middle of the street. But it's safe and there are few cars. In Cuba, no one is going anywhere.

When I return to this neighborhood two days later, it's during the day and large green shutters protect the insides of the homes from the oppressive heat of the afternoon. An onshore breeze slides into the rooms through slits. I have a feeling that nothing here is absolute, that everything exists in dusky maybes.

I have managed to summon up enough Spanish to tell the woman on the telephone that I am from the United States, from Nuevo Mexico, indeed from Santa Fe and that I have gifts for her. There is a quiet pause. I begin repeating my bare bones greeting, thinking maybe she didn't understand me. But she did. She tells me she will arrange to come by my hotel in the morning.

The next day at the appointed time, a rusted, non-descript car pulls up, wedging between tour buses and taxis. A man jumps out of the driver's seat and opens the door for her, carefully helping her out of the car. Somehow we recognize each other. She calls me Kusel. I call her señora. She is 92 years old and frail.

She slides her hand into the crook of my arm and together we slowly walk into the hotel. That's when things started falling apart. Cubans, it seems, are not allowed to mingle with tourists. The hotel security won't let her inside. It's against the rules, they tell me. They are on the alert for thievery. It's for my own protection.

I feel her grip tighten on my arm. This must be a mistake. This woman isn't a thief. She is an elder and as such demands respect and reverence. I ask the guard if this is why he fought the revolution; to keep old women out of hotels. He doesn't blink. He repeats the rules.

I switch to Spanish and ask him the same question. The point is moot, and the señora and I return to the car. I make arrangements to deliver the suitcase to her on the street, away from the hotel.

Two days later, she calls me and invites me to her home. Although I have difficulty finding her apartment during the day, there are people in the streets who are more than willing to help. Cubans have this affinity toward Americans, or north Americans as they call us.

Walking in the streets, strangers would come up and speak to me first in French. When I shook my head, they would tentatively ask, "English?" My reply of "Estados Unidos" never failed to illicit a wide smile, usually accompanied with a story of some long-ago relative living in New York or Miami.

I climb the two flights of stairs, which open directly into her apartment. Her hand is warm as she reaches out and pulls me inside with surprising force. She settles me in one of two rocking chairs and then the questions begin.

She is wearing lipstick today and her hair is swept back away from her face, revealing a high forehead and wonderful, pronounced cheekbones. For someone in her ninth decade, she looks remarkably spry and healthy.

She is glad for the suitcase filled with soap and shampoo but wants to know about how I came to deliver them to her. She wants to know our connection, and I really can't tell her because I don't know.

But she is looking to me for answers about someone she hasn't seen in nearly 40 years and someone I knew for only 10 minutes. So, I look into her beautiful, open face, and I lie to her. Her relative is living a wonderful life in Santa Fe. She lives in a very large house. Her life is filled with friends and music. She drives a new car, and has a good job.

Have I overstepped the boundaries of decency and trust? But when she takes my hand and holds it to her heart and tells me that now she is filled with a feeling of contentment, I push away my own questions.

She has lived in this house for more than 45 years, she says. After the revolution, people kept their homes, only now they belonged to the state, but then everything does. Even the cars they drive.

Stepping into her home was like walking into a pocket time forgot. Whatever was there in 1959 when Castro marched out of the mountains and into Havana, is still there today. A Moorish chandelier echoes the shape of the arched windows that look out toward the ocean. But there is no bulb in the fixture. Electricity is difficult. Blackouts persist.

The house has running water. The water groans through old pipes and trickles coldly out of the faucets. Paint is peeling off the walls. The ceilings are water-stained, turned a tobacco brown with time. But there is no paint available for repairs. So she sits, looks out toward the ocean, and beyond the horizon, toward America. She walks to a table and picks up a framed photograph. The woman in the picture is young and beautiful.

"That's me," she says in a rusty English. "When I was a young girl."

Before she retired, she was an educator. When various members of her family left, part of the 150,000-person migration that fled the island, she stayed behind. Cuba is her home, she says proudly.

Things may be difficult, but there are few complaints. Everyone's education is paid for. So is housing and health care. The average worker earns 300 pesos a month. About $14. There is a thriving black market where Cubans can buy the foods their ration books don't cover with dollars earned from tourists or received from relatives in the United States as officials seemingly turn a blind eye.

I have given her an envelope with money, but it is never mentioned. Every house has its ears; every block, its selected watchman from the Committee for the Defense of the Revolution who watches over the safety of the neighborhood.

Later, before I leave, unseen I slide more money beneath the lace doily on a side table.

I know we will never meet again.

Digging Digital

I won't say that I was dragged kicking and screaming into the digital revolution, but receiving a digital camera for Christmas has caused me to stop and think.

I'm of two minds about digital. First, it's great having a camera that takes photos I could email to my parents, showing them how normal my life is in Santa Fe so they can stop pestering me with such questions as has the road outside the house been paved yet and whether or not local stores still accept pesos.

On the other hand, digital pushes me further into debt to a virtual conspiracy of saving something, but not really saving it at all.

Ostensibly, one of the best features of going digital is the ability for instant editing, which means you can not only immediately see what the picture looks like, but also can decide if you want to keep it.

So far, photographs of my average life in Santa Fe have included: Picture of the cat rolled over on his back with his feet in the air

Picture of Boomer the Basset lying on his back with his feet in the air

Picture of bearded collie that has so much hair people often talk to the wrong end.

"What's wrong with those animals?" my mother asked after she received my email.

"They're fine, Ma. They're just relaxed."

"How come there are no pictures of you? "

"No pictures of me because I'm the one taking the pictures."

"Well, you'd think that after putting a man on the moon, they would invent cameras smart enough to take pictures on their own."

So, now that you can see where I got my advanced logic and reasoning skills, let's move right along to where the pictures are kept.

Actually, they are not kept. They're stored, usually on the hard drive of your computer or an auxiliary device like CD or Zip disk. But often they're deleted because our computers are not powerful enough to store such large files.

This brings us to the foible of digital. If we delete the photographs, having never printed them, this means that for generations to come, history will be bereft of accurate records showing what we looked like and what we enjoyed doing during these years.

Combine this with the lack of letters, diaries and personal papers we will no longer be leaving behind, having consigned our lives to the lure of the virtual, and you have the recipe for a shadow generation.

As for the destruction of documents, I wonder how much of history in this country will never see the light of day because of an adherence to the adage, when in doubt, shred it.

Gamboling at the Casino

It was the dead part of the afternoon. At 2:30, the wind was blowing hot and parched. Camel Rock Casino offered an air-conditioned diversion. But I didn't just happen in there. I planned my visit after reading about compulsive gambling, which is more of a problem in a poor state like New Mexico than in a state where people have money.

It is estimated that five percent of the gamblers in the state are problem gamblers. The national level is three percent.

The problem of compulsive gambling in New Mexico is growing, especially for women because, the story said, women gamble to escape loneliness and pain.

"Women are the most at-risk population, with the risk factors being poverty, loneliness, bad relationship conditions, domestic violence and chemical dependency," said Daniel Blackwood of the New Mexico Council on Problem Gambling, which despite the official sounding name, is a private, non-profit community-based organization.

Blackwood is both the program's executive director and a counselor who works with compulsive gamblers.

"In a state where there are poor economic conditions, the higher the (incidence) of compulsive gambling. In this state, chemical dependency, poverty and domestic violence are linked to problem gambling.

"The percentage of women who tell us they are victims of domestic abuse or suffer from an alcohol or drug addiction has grown.

"In the first quarter of 2000, about 11 percent of the (help-line) callers said they had been victims of domestic abuse, compared to six percent in the last quarter of 1999."

The casino parking lot is more than a quarter full. All but four of the license plates read " New Mexico."

Inside, the air conditioning is humming. Two men are at the

roulette wheel, but most people are sitting on stools in front of slot machines that shoot off seductive neon winks and spirals of sound

"This is how I do it," said Minnie, who told me she was from Tesuque Pueblo. "You put two quarters in at a time, and then you hit the spin button like this, punchpunchpunch."

She was standing in front of an Elvis slot. If you win, The King sings something. She didn't win.

There are four phases of compulsive gambling: Winning, losing, desperation and recovery. Compulsion is sandwiched somewhere between winning and losing.

"Sixty-nine percent of phone calls to the hotline are from women 35 years and older," Blackwood said. "Some call, afraid about what their husbands will do to them (when they find out about the gambling). Others call asking what to do; some are suicidal; but most are depressed, anxious."

I watched Minnie fishing around in her leather purse, looking for the odd quarter. I pointed out there were two quarters in the bottom of the slot tray. She told me she didn't see well anymore.

As she inserted them into the slot, she began talking, telling me about herself, about her husband who died seven years ago, about the kind of life she has now.

The second most at risk group of compulsive gamblers? Elderly women. The reason? Loneliness.

The number for the Helpline at the New Mexico Council on Problem Gambling is (800) 572-1142. The number for the U.S. Gambling hotline is (800) 522-4700.

Despite all these numbers, the odds are not in your favor.

Re-Unionizing

Now that my zip code has changed, I'm not getting all of my mail. Strangely, however, the invitation to my high school reunion managed to make it through.

I was in high school so long ago, the planning committee can't remember how many years we're celebrating and lumped my class in with a bunch of others.

I attended a reunion a number of years ago. There were some poignant moments, but mainly the same people who planned the reunion were former cheerleaders and prom queens. Some behaviors die hard.

I have a confession. I always read the acknowledgements in the front of books to see if someone I went to high school with ever amounted to anything. So far, nada, but I keep looking.

We didn't do drugs in school. It was so many years ago, most drugs were still legal. Sure, we had our problems. I remember at the football games, the cheerleaders would yell fight and the stands would empty.

Meanwhile, the invitation noted festivities would be held in Odin's Hall, which was a fancy name they gave to the multipurpose room.

The last time I was there was on prom night and the decorating committee had hung Christmas trees upside-down to make the place look festive.

Odin's Hall also was where school assemblies were held. You remember the scene—teachers standing in back of the room, arms folded across their chests looking like their knickers were in a knot. Something happened at assemblies. Even the best kids would become screw-ups. Maybe it was about being part of a group.

I decided to call my old high school boyfriend to see if he wanted to go to the reunion with me. After all, we did go to the prom together and swore our love would be true forever and ever. Well, at least we did keep in touch.

I dialed his number and his wife of 100 years answered.

"Hi, is Gary there?" I asked.

"Yeah, I'll wake him. He's sleeping in front the TV. The game is on."

"Don't you want to know who's calling?"

"Who cares. You're probably selling something anyway."

"I'm his old high school girlfriend," I blurted.

There was a pause, and I heard her suck in her breath, and then let it out again slowly. Actually, it sounded like a hiss.

"You don't say. What was he like?" she asked.

"Oh, lots of fun. We'd do crazy things like fly to Mexico for breakfast and San Francisco for dinner."

"Doesn't sound like my husband. He hasn't been off the couch for the last 15 years. I think you have the wrong number," she said, hanging up.

High Cost of Working at Home

After more than a year of writing a column, I've been rethinking this working at home and telecommunicating thing.

For one, it's quite costly. It also takes quite a lot of time, even though I'm not actually going anywhere.

Let's look at the numbers and compare.

Working in town:

Wake up at 5:30 a.m. Feed the animals. Bathe. Dress in clean, well-pressed clothing. Run out the door without making coffee or eating breakfast.

Cost of driving back and forth to work in an under-powered, gas-guzzling SUV, $20 per week. Cost of one cup of designer coffee per day for five days, $28.25. Cost of eating lunch at one of the trendy, over-priced Downtown restaurants specializing in big attitude and small portions, $34.

The total for the week is about $153.

Working at home:

Wake up at 5:30 a.m. Feed the animals. Still dark outside. Go back to bed. Wake up at 7:30 a.m. Feed animals because I've forgotten I've already fed them and they look hungry. Take a bath. Spend a lot of time looking in the mirror and wondering where all the wrinkles and gray hair came from overnight.

Open closet. Get depressed because clothing has somehow shrunk while hanging in the closet and nothing fits anymore. Unfortunately, there is no one around to talk to about this problem.

Put pajamas back on. Think about going back to bed, but decide to try to make a stab at the day. Do not make the bed since I will probably want to nap later.

Brew pot of special tea mail-ordered from TibetUbet.com. Cost of one cup $226.39, not including the special Tibet prayer bell also purchased online at ringyourchimes.com.

Read the newspaper, which I have to pay for. Read the newspaper again, this time with a red marker.

Turn on computer and read email. Search for foreign newspapers online. Note interesting article on new restaurants in the International Herald Tribune. Call up skyauction.com. Book trip to Paris. Cost $1,545. No money left over for hotel. Make note to meet someone on the plane.

Computer too slow. Lacks memory. Buy new computer from outpost.com. Tell them I need it today by five p.m. Cost: $899.

Begin pacing office. Rug looks worn where I've been pacing. Order new one from rugsBme.com. Cost: $3,000.

Begin thinking about lunch. Walk to refrigerator to see if strangers have broken into the house and left some food inside.

Consider eating old apple found behind microwave oven. Decide instead to make Appalachian apple core doll to sell on eBay.

Instant message my parents. Ask if it's too late to move home. Work on guilt angle. Tell them other kids are moving home every day.

Brew new cup of tea with leaves imported by OuterMongolia.com and carried to secret shipment point by yak. Cost of loose tea for one cup: $167, not including yak butter smears on outside of shipping carton, which were extra.

Read newspaper again looking for minutiae that might make good column, paying special notice to quotes from local politicos. Forget it. No one would ever believe I could be that obtuse.

Make appointment on therapist.com. Go back to bed.

This is a Real Alert

Hormone replacement therapy may be bad for women? Did you see that headline in the paper? Is this one of those stories they trot out on a slow news days when nothing else in the world is going on?

Or are they just flat-out crazy? Clearly, they don't know what they're dealing with here.

Do anything. Anything. Root canals. Ingrown toenail removal. Botox withdrawal. But don't touch my hormones.

At first I thought it was one of President Bush's stupid ploys to get rid of Bin Laden.

You want to get rid of Bin Laden? Forget the marines. They can't hold a candle to WWH—Women Without Hormones. Women of the United States unite. We'll root out Bin Laden in two days.

We'll find him. We'll rip his head off. Pull that beard out, hair by hair. Just don't fool with us. This is not a joke. This is a real alert.

I was so upset, I called my mother.

"Hey, Ma, did you hear?"

"You calling me Ma? Me? Your mother with a capital M? Don't even fool with me this morning."

I could tell she had read the morning paper. I heard it in the tone of her voice, in the grinding of her teeth. I knew even then she was ripping off bits of newsprint and rolling them into makeshift bullets.

"Where's dad?" I asked.

"Who?"

"My father. Where is he?"

"He's hiding. He's locked himself in the bathroom."

"Why the bathroom?" I asked.

"It's the only room with a lock. But I'm about to fix that."

"You're picking the lock?"

"No. I'm ripping off the whole door. And when I finish with that, I'm starting on the refrigerator."

"Wow. That's cool. You're taking the door off the refrigerator?"

"No. I'm eating all the ice cream."

"Way to go, Ma."

"Did I hear you call me Ma? Did I just warn you about that? I'm flying in."

Now, I've got to pause here, explain a few things. As long as I can remember, my mother always told me that no matter where I was in the world, if I were in trouble, she'd get on a plane and rescue me.

"You want me to pick you up in Albuquerque?" I asked dutifully.

"What Albuquerque? I said I was flying in," she snarled.

"How?" the word escaped my lips before I could snap them shut.

"Two days without hormones," she blurted. "I can do anything. I'm flying in. And then we're going to take care of that putz Bin Laden."

"Right on, Mother."

"Why are you still using those out-of-date Sixties phrases with me?" she barked.

I sighed. "So what are we going to do after we off Bin Laden?"

"What's to do? We'll go shopping."

Road Dreams

Romance comes to mind. Followed by vintage dreams of the open road and a deep nostalgic ache for better times.

This is the mindset that nibbles at the spokes of your brain when you see a photograph of the Indian Motorcycle.

To see one in person and catch your reflection in the sexy curvaceous sweep of the fenders is like falling in love with a classic mystique.

Not just anyone rode an Indian. It took a special person with that rare ability to transcend time and fall in love with those flare fenders and studded leather saddlebags with fringe that danced in the wind.

Michael Breeding was only 19 when he made the commitment and become one of those exceptional few.

He paid $35 for a modified 1953 Indian Chief in a creampuff color combo of turquoise and white. He's still got it.

It's parked in his Santa Fe workshop right next to a 1947 stealth black Indian with a sidecar rig.

Suspended on a workbench, a 1951 Chief Bobber named Yellow Dog is tricked out with a chrome gearshift stick inlaid with the likeness of the trademark Indian head.

"I make my own parts for these," Breeding said, quickly adding that he doesn't make bikes, restore them or service them for other people.

"Everything you see in here is mine, including that 1951 Vincent Black Shadow over in the corner."

The guy with eyes the color of wild New Mexico skies lives and breathes motorcycles. He doesn't just make parts, he fashions them with meticulous care and precision.

"I'm making Indian Motorcycle parts the way a jeweler makes jewelry," Breeding said in his soft Texas drawl. "I use the lost wax method. The tools are heat treated."

All the tools and parts he reproduces carry a foundry mark, mold number and raised part number. I found myself hungering for an Indian wrench even though I don't own a bike.

Just being in Breeding's workshop, where the perfume of WD-40 lingers in the air, is a total experience, right down to the wall plastered with vintage Land of Enchantment license plates.

There's something about being in a workshop with a master craftsman who takes pride in his work that made me feel alive and happy.

On one wall, a bank of carefully labeled plastic drawers yielded a variety of acorn, castle and hex nuts the size of a small fingernail.

Against another, were Breeding's collection of motorcycle jackets, including an oiled cotton Barbour International, with special pockets for maps and motorcycle tools.

"It's a tight world, this Indian Motorcycle group," Breeding said. "The factory closed last month, but I still make 450 parts, including Indian insignia belt buckles and jewelry pins."

The one element not being reproduced is the Indian head that rides on the front fender and glows like warm ivory.

Some things are better left alone.

What's in a Name?

Authorities were wringing hands and necks over exactly who is going to claim responsibility for the mistaken release of all 600 of the Antonio Martinez's registered in the correction system's computers.

One particular Martinez walked out of a privately owned Estancia jail after being mistakenly released over a mix-up due to the celebration of one of his several birthdays.

It seems Martinez was released on June 10, 1900, but the confusion went unnoticed until another Antonio Martinez, who shared a birthday with 599 other inmates with the same name, was delivered to a court hearing in Santa Fe on his birthday exactly one hundred years later.

Henry Valdez, who is celebrating his 438th consecutive year as Santa Fe County District Attorney, thus, proving once again that name recognition not record is what counts during an election, said his office could not comment on the investigation until "it was complete," which is not expected to be during our life time.

Antonio Martinez was originally being held in the Santa Fe Jail awaiting his right to a speedy trial.

Officials began to get suspicious when yet another Antonio Martinez, this one a third grade student at a still-to-be-determined charter school, was reported missing from his fourth period class. He later reportedly showed up at the shopping mall in Estancia, which was having a sale on school uniforms.

Correction officials from throughout the state quickly went on record claiming absolutely no responsibility in the matter. However, all agreed it would now take an act of God or a note from a parent before any inmate with the initials A.M. would be released from any facility in the world. Period. So there.

A search of the New Mexico correction department's computers turned up 527 more individuals identified as A. Martinez, all of whom were celebrating their birthdays around the same time.

This fact was discovered after prison officials complained about having to sing happy birthday so many times in a row.

District Attorney Valdez said his office was looking into the problem of having to supply birthday cakes and candles to so many A. Martinez's.

Valdez said no one from his office would be allowed to comment on the fact that all Antonio Martinez's had similar birthdays until after contacting one of the psychics he'd seen advertised on late-night TV.

He denied, however, that he was sending for the complete CD set of rock 'n' roll oldies, also advertised on TV but absolutely not available in any store.

Meanwhile, when asked what he was doing while he was walking around free, Antonio Martinez said he had spent time in Las Vegas (the other Las Vegas) getting married and playing the slots.

Still another Antonio Martinez told authorities that he had registered to vote four or five times in the same election in Rio Arriba County.

The Antonio Martinez who was allegedly apprehended while shopping with his mother at the mall, was released pending notification of his homeroom teacher.

Keeping Us Safe for Democracy

When it comes to picking out names for newly invented offices, the feds haven't a clue.

Take the Office of Homeland Security. When I first heard the name, I thought a new part of the old Savings & Loan scandal had surfaced.

Something this big calls for clear thinking, which is why I'm here. Someone needs to keep us safe for democracy. Or is it from democracy? Prepositions are always tricky.

Office of Pervasive Mediocrity: This office has grown like topsy and integrated through our entire society.

Office of Inferior Posterior: A much-needed constitutional oversight team to help us look over our shoulders and remember the Bill of Rights as it used to be.

Office of Checks and Stripes: Replaces the old system of checks and balances, which proved to be just too pesky. Besides, it didn't know how to dress.

Office of Parsimonious Reform: Keeps the public busy thinking the $300 tax rebate really meant something, proving that not only can you fool all of the people all of the time, but that they also come cheap.

Office of Farcical Fulmination: People employed to grouse about things that ensures their own employment. Since redundancy in government is the norm, any move toward consolidation will necessarily fail.

Office of Campaign Reform: Using the 100th Monkey Theory, this office is busy proving that all you need is one monkey talking about campaign reform before the entire population begins believing it can happen, but of course never does.

Office of Inter-Galactic Gadgetry: The so-called War Toys Office. Staff comprised of men wearing a variety of uniforms from the odd college tie to the full-star general. Meets in an uncarpeted room where the guys try out a variety of mechanical things that explode and make a lot of noise.

Office of Audacious Alert: This office has carte blanche to pick out people who look differently, including anyone having dark skin, dark eyes and an accent, and arrest them without due process.

Office of Corporate Condolences: Gee, we're sorry for all the problems but since we're so multinational we simply can't keep track of where one corporation begins and another ends. In fact, they don't.

Office of Car Pool: In order to keep us focused on all things military, this office is working overtime to sell the public on driving brightly painted HumVees, retrofitted for friendly civilian use with fuzzy dice.

Office of Lower-End of the Gene Pool: You used to be able to easily pick these people out in a crowd because they didn't have necks and sported large educational gaps. But this is no longer the case. Due to genetic engineering and the ensuing dumbing down of society, these people now look like the rest of us, although an uncommon number have been elected to higher office.

It Just Depends

I'm sure you've heard the rumors, but I swear they're true. I am going to be in the Winter Olympics.

Yeah, I know, you're wondering, "Wow, she's so cool, is there anything she can't do?" Absolutely not.

Although it's been years since I've actually gone up the mountain to ski, I'm not about to let that stop me. After all, I can't spell and that doesn't stop me from writing.

Come on and I'll plug in my MP3 player so you hear what the announcers had to say about my near qualifying run.

"This is purely amazing, I mean look at that hair. It's white. You can't tell the top of her head from the snow."

"That's right, Bob. Word on the circuit is that she'll stop at nothing to confuse the issue."

"Look at her in that snowsuit. I have to say right here that I've never seen gravity be that cruel to any one person. I didn't know Lycra stretched in so many directions at once. Oh-oh, here she goes into that half-inverted 350 casserole."

"I know, Bob, it's hard to imagine that just until last week the only casserole she knew about was the kind you put into the oven at 350."

"Oh, man, that was so insane, she just went into a double back flip, coming out of it into a flat-on belly flop, combining two sports into one-swimming with snowboarding. That was totally wacky. A full ballerina factor. A real switcheroo. A super-pike medalist couldn't have hit it better."

"Our viewers at home are probably wondering right now, just how she keeps that momentum. She's on fire. But wait, she's not stopping at the end of the speed and stylin' tunnel, she's going directly for the lodge. She's disappeared right into the bar. Let's see if we can catch up with her.

"Hey, Denise, that was totally awesome. How do you do this kind of speed at your age?"

"Depends."

"Depends on what?"

"Depends. I wear Depends. Truth is I usually like to, you know, sit on the couch, kick back with a brewski."

"So you were telling us how you got up to that terrific speed."

"It really wasn't on purpose. I mean, I don't even like snow. I just got going so fast and couldn't stop, so I closed my eyes."

"You mean you turned those flips in the air with your eyes closed."

"You don't think I could do something like that with my eyes open?"

"Tell us how did you get into snowboarding?"

"I didn't want to make too much of an investment and I already had this boogie board left over from my Beach Boy days."

"There are people who say you're past your prime. That you're too old for a hotshot sport. Do you have anything you want to say to them?"

"Depends."

Netherworld of Technology

Welcome to Santa Fe, that dead zone. That netherworld where cell phones and regular wired phones simply don't work.

So what if earlier this week the FTC passed a ruling making it easier for cell phone users to change their regular home telephone number to their cell phones?

At my house, we have to find something that actually carries a voice signal, although the idea of having to memorize one less number sounds promising.

First, there's your Social Security number. Next comes the pin number for your bank account. The pin number for your online banking. The pin number for credit cards. If you have more than one credit card, which I don't, that means there're more numbers to retain.

I'm sure I'm not the only one who lives in a dead zone where cell phone signals die somewhere between the driveway and the front door and where wired telephones are spotty at best.

Before going to Europe last spring, I rented a satellite phone guaranteed to work all over the world. It didn't work in Santa Fe.

Sometimes the only person to get through to me is my mother, who manages to do this with or without a phone.

This kind of communication is possible between all mothers and daughters and should be studied closely by telephone delivery companies.

"It's your mother. We're coming for Thanksgiving," she shouted.

"Mom, how are you doing this?" I shouted into my empty hand. Shouting while on a long distance call is something I learned from my parents that they learned from their parents. Today, in the era of fiber optics, we still shout.

"We're flying in," came the reply.

"No, not that. I mean how are you talking to me when none of my phones work?"

"That's easy. It's the flying in that's more difficult," she yelled.

Do mothers lose this special ability for contact as you get older? The answer is no.

In fact, there are some sayings all mothers learn, regardless of the ethnic culture. I call these momisms and they are with us for the rest of our lives, beginning with the first time we heard our mothers' voices coming out of our mouths.

"If it were a snake, it would have bitten you" is a popular momism. Another is, "Eat this, it's going bad."

"This is going to hurt me more than it hurts you." "Close the door, we are not heating up the neighborhood." "Where do you think you're going looking like that?"

And the ever-popular, "Don't look at me in that tone of voice."

Then I heard something new coming out of my mother's mouth.

"Your father and I are going to Canada for drugs," my mother announced.

If I had told her I was going to Canada for drugs, I would have been grounded for the rest of this life and the next.

Ready for the Psychic Network

Since last April, the Psychic Network has hired 15 New York City welfare recipients as psychics. They also offered on-the-job training in tarot reading and looking into the future.

But now the New York City Human Resources Administration (remember when places like that were called the Unemployment Office and everyone knew what you were talking about when you mentioned it by name?) has announced it no longer was placing unemployed welfare recipients into jobs with the Psychic Network.

This decision was not based on the former welfare recipients' ability to tell fortunes.

In fact, it was never revealed why this decision was made. It seems no one complained about that. What I want to know is how you train someone to look into the future. The closest I ever got was when my mother admonished me to wear clean underwear because I might be in a car wreck.

But now that New York no longer is supplying psychics, I think the network should come to Santa Fe to recruit. In fact, they would have no problem finding applicants here, especially since the Psychic Network is paying $10 an hour, plus bonuses.

Now in Santa Fe, where some employers pay $6.25 an hour and are wondering why they can't hire dedicated people who might want to spend the rest of their life flipping burgers, this amount is a positive windfall.

Since experience also counts, please take this test:

If you have been a psychic in a past life, give yourself five points.

If the adult parent of your inner child is in a tarot dependency program, give yourself six points.

If you have been to Taos in the last year, please deduct seven points. If you heard the hum, add three.

If you know the exact location of the Pleiades when you were born, give yourself four points.

If you have had an astrological sign change operation in the past year, give yourself five points.

In other news, the computer glitch that shut down the Motor Vehicle Department offices throughout the state Monday will absolutely not effect the status of the temporary registration cards issued to some drivers after the company responsible for producing new license tags missed its deadline.

Meanwhile, it should be mentioned that the temporary registration cards look exactly like the registration cards that should have been mailed back to the MVD along with your check covering the cost of the new tags.

If you registered for your new tags online, you are still in possession of the original registration card. Any attempt to confuse these two cards is punishable by imprisonment for the rest of this life and the next, just as soon as the state figures out to which private prison facility to send you.

Since you know who you are, you could save everyone a lot of time and aggravation by turning yourself in to the authorities at the Santa Fe Police Department, which, by the way, is still looking for that $8 reported missing from the petty cash drawer in early January.

Rumors that the missing $8 is the exact amount the county pays sheriffs deputies per hour should be taken with a grain of salt.

The Santa Fe County Sheriff's Department said they might soon have up to 18 vacancies because some deputies have left in search of more lucrative salaries.

Officials would neither confirm nor deny that some deputies were sending their applications to the Psychic Network, which pays $10 an hour, plus bonuses.

Sanitizing Abusive Behavior

I rebel when it comes to using euphemisms to cloak habits and sanitize abusive behavior.

The term racial profiling is near the top. It's a phrase much in vogue these days to describe how we react to certain people. But make no mistake; the words are but a fancy way of disguising prejudice and racism.

Racial profiling is a fundamental violation of liberty, and decency demands we abhor such thoughts.

In the wake of the tragedy of terrorism, we have been warned we are in danger of our civil liberties undergoing erosion and compromise.

We must be careful to guard against succumbing to the peril of losing the very essence that helps make us human, our compassion for others.

It is sad and unconscionable to look with circumspect on men and women who appear to be of Middle Eastern descent. Didn't we learn anything in WWII with relocating Japanese-Americans into concentration camps because they looked different?

One of the Sikhs who works at Sunrise Market said he is feeling jittery after some of his brethren were attacked in Arizona because they "looked Arab."

"Do you think I should display my citizenship papers near the cash register?" he asked.

If it gets to that, my friends, we must all display proof of citizenship. There is no justification for singling out people who look a certain way. This is not what America is about.

Yet the sentiments to separate minorities for special notice seems to be on our lips after the terrorist attacks of September 11.

We are being painfully confronted with behavior we know is wrong.

Many people have expressed revulsion at the spate of attacks on Muslims, as well as Sikhs and Hindus.

Not only is our ignorance showing, but our inhumanity as well. A recent nationwide Gallup poll conducted by CNN and USA Today showed that Americans were supporting special treatment for those of Arab descent, with 58 percent favoring more intensive security checks for Arabs, including those who are United States citizens, compared with other travelers.

Forty-nine percent said they favored special identification cards for such people, and 32 percent wanted "special surveillance" for them.

Some believed there was no justification for racial profiling. Others said they believed everyone should be treated the same way. Still others said they were consciously attempting to put aside snap judgments they were making about others based on racial differences.

It's lining up to be a hard fight. But it's an honorable fight, and one that will eventually prove our merit as a people.

By the time you read this, I will have gotten on a plane for a month-long trip to Guatemala to live with a family and study Spanish to satisfy a longing to hear the old stories of Northern New Mexico while there still are elders here to tell them.

When I get on that plane, will I have the fortitude to act out the strength of my belief that we are all one people in one world?

Defending the Homeland

These are the days of silences and whispers. These are nervous, tenuous times, quickly becoming fraught with fright.

These are days of Total Information Awareness, a mega computer wielded by John Poindexter spying on you and me giving the government the instant ability to look in on our email, monitor our bank books, all in the name of defending America against terrorism, and all without a search warrant.

Ordinary people are becoming increasingly afraid that what we are saying and writing is being recorded and noted somewhere.

"I find I'm second-guessing myself," a friend whispered while we were having coffee. "I was emailing a friend in Germany, making excuses for what's going on in this country. But I began questioning whether or not I should send it.

"We've already been warned that the Office of Homeland Defense can monitor our email and monitor phone calls," she continued, nervously looking over her shoulder.

When I first heard the term "Homeland Defense," I thought it was part of the savings and loan scandal rearing its ugly head once more.

I was wrong. It was worse.

Sadly, the more I listened the more I thought what a wonderful public relations ploy it was to take loaded words close to our hearts like "home" and "land" and infuse them up with visions of fear.

And believe me, I am as frightened as the next person when I think of terrorism. But I also am more frightened about silence and the kinds of terrorism that are blanketing our civil rights as American citizens, smothering those same rights we were taught to hold to be self-evident.

These are the very truths that were protected in the Privacy Act of 1974, which was passed to protect us by limiting governmental access to our personal information.

It was that law that put the FBI in charge of domestic intelligence and further limited that organization on spying on political and religious groups without first providing that those groups were involved in a crime.

It also stopped such agencies as the CIA and the National Security Agency from listening in on you and me.

We cannot afford to allow paranoia to constrict our throats.

When we have to think twice about expressing our thoughts, something is very wrong.

When we have to silence our words because we are afraid someone will overhear us and misconstrue what we are saying, something is very wrong.

It should be a crime that the erosion of our civil liberties is permitted to hide behind the names of the heroes who died on 9/11.

This is the season of giving, and the most important gift we can embrace is the gift of free speech.

We must ask ourselves if our silent nights are really holy nights.

Placing Blame

It's a crime we live in such a litigineous society. Someone should be sued.

We've lost the ability to be responsible for our own actions. There needs to be some kind of reward for working at placing blame elsewhere.

Here are some court settlements that never were printed in the paper, mostly because they never happened.

But, of course, that's just the point. They could have, and just because they didn't doesn't mean someone should not collect a large amount of money for what might have been.

A 45-year-old man was awarded $4.5 million after claiming he lost his ability to roller skate after being yelled at by a roller rink attendant when he was 10 years old while attempting to return a pair of shoe skates without the laces.

A woman who claimed a Wal-Mart Greeter told her to have a good day and then smiled at her was awarded an undisclosed amount of money after a jury decided that it would be OK if the greeter had told her to have a good day or smiled, but not both.

A man caught stealing tools from one of Santa Fe's attractive box stores was awarded $15 million after a jury decided that the store detective who caught him had interrupted his ability to earn money by fencing stolen property.

A woman who asked passers-by how to get to the library was awarded $65 billion by a jury, which claimed that knowing exactly how to find her way to the library denied her of the right to wander around town aimlessly.

Two middle-aged men were awarded a lot of money after claiming that because they were not chosen to serve as alter boys when they were younger, they now are being prevented from suing the Catholic Church.

A man who told police someone broke into his car while parked on a downtown street was awarded $47 thousand even though he later admitted he didn't have a car. The jury decided that if he did have a car, it would probably have been burglarized because that's what happens to a lot of cars.

A woman who claimed that she no longer shops at one of Santa Fe's overpriced natural food stores because it was too expensive received a hefty cash settlement after proving that vegetables were people, too.

A boy and a girl who were selling lemon-aid and cookies in front of their home located on a cul-de-sac successfully sued their parents, claiming that by being forced to live in a safe and quiet neighborhood with little traffic inhibited their ability to earn big bucks.

A woman who showed up for a hay ride at an area horse stable was awarded $59 thousand after the stable cancelled the hayride, which the jury said denied the woman her right to have an allergic reaction to hay.

Clarifying a Few Tax Issues

Tax season is perking its way into our collective consciousness, so it's time for me to clarify a few issues.

First of all, 501(c) 3 is not the name of blue jeans sold by Levis. This is important to know because in Santa Fe, the first thing people want to know about you is your 501(c) 3, which is your non-profit number, thereby turning your date into a tax deduction.

The next thing they want to know is who is your umbrella organization. Umbrellas have nothing to do with a rainy day, unless your group was saving for one when the stock market turned bullish, bearish and brutish all at once.

People want to know about your umbrella because they want to know if there is space underneath for them as well. Do not give your Social Security number to strangers.

Secondly, the Short Form may also be used by tall people. That's because due to an oversight, there is no Tall Form for income tax and the government wouldn't want any of us to feel left out.

To learn if you qualify for the Short Form, which will save you a bunch of money in your over-priced CPA's office where they use the same kind of computer you use at home, apply this handy formula:

Multiply your part-time jobs by the highest amount in the catastrophic illness rider on your insurance policy.

If any of these numbers end in zero, something is sadly wrong; however, you might be able to make up a new Social Security number when you file your taxes, and start life over as a rich person.

In the event that the IRS actually catches on and investigates this new number, which is highly unlikely, do not contest the issue.

Simply tell them you have so many PIN numbers to remember these days, that you just got confused.

If that doesn't work, plead forgetfulness. A lot of us are forgetting more and more these days.

You can arrive at your new Social Security number by dividing the number of pets' names you are using for PIN numbers by the amount of money you spend on pet treats in a month.

If you have decided to use the Intermediate Form, which is new this year, please disregard everything you've ever been told in your life.

The Intermediate Form is for people with intermediate intelligence. If your local tax office has run out of these forms, ask for an automatic extension for paying your taxes, and then go home and take to your bed. Period. So there.

The Intermediate Form was devised by the government because they know that since the last presidential election all bets are off and a lot of us are thinking of blowing off this whole tax thing anyway. This form is a last-ditch attempt at keeping us in the fold.

In the spirit of Questioning Authority, the Intermediate Form doesn't ask direct questions. It tricks you into thinking the government cares. Here are some examples.

1. Do you think you paid too much money in taxes last year? Enter the number here.
2. Do you think you are entitled to universal health care? If so, enter the amount you paid the last time you visited Urgent Care because you don't have a family doctor.
3. If you live in Santa Fe, are you claiming an automatic deduction for your inner-child?

Tax Rebate Debate

Let's talk tax rebates. It seems that not everyone is going to get one. But on the other hand, some people are.

Lucky for you, I understand matters of high finance and have learned to handle large amounts of cash due to my well-paying job at The New Mexican.

The first thing to remember is that refunds are based on your 2000 taxes, not this year's taxes even if you promise to spend a lot of money this year and save the nation's economy single-handed.

If you are a married couple who has received a refund from your 2000 taxes you might be eligible for something.

If, on the other hand, you have not filed your Federal Income Tax for 2000 because of the extension granted to victims of the Cerro Grande

Fire, you may be in for a surprise because if you think we at the IRS are going to let you slide for a couple of months, you should be reminded that hell has not frozen over for some time.

In the event that hell does freeze over sometime this summer, you may be eligible for some loose change.

People living in the Santa Fe area should not expect a refund at all because they don't earn enough money to even consider getting some back.

If you are a single person living in Santa Fe and work in the city's well-paying tourist industry, you will not receive a refund no matter how many part-time jobs you hold.

If you are a gay couple living in Santa Fe, you are not eligible for a refund no matter how nicely your home is decorated.

If you are a straight couple living in Santa Fe, you're probably lying. There are only two straight couples living in Santa Fe.

If you are not gay, straight, single or married, you may figure out your refund using the following handy reference table:

If you work only 39 hours a week because your employer is too cheap to offer you health insurance and benefits that would be due you if you worked a 40-hour week, deduct 25 percent of your reported gross income. This should be easy since a lot of us earn gross amounts of money anyway.

If you hitchhike to work because your car died last year on Apodaca Hill and disappeared into a pothole, add $3.75 transportation credit.

If you have a second home in Santa Fe, you will automatically receive a hefty refund because of the charitable ways you support locals.

If you are self-employed and have not had a vacation in six years and have not had enough money to get out of Santa Fe for five of those years, tough nuggies.

Next time, remember to vote.

Because We Care About Your Business

Although I receive my email through *The New Mexican*, Earthlink is my dial-up number, if you know what I mean.

If you don't know what I mean, it doesn't matter, because I don't understand it either. These are just words I've heard bandied about by the computer techs at the newspaper.

In fact, words like dial-up, bounce and echo have taken on new meanings in my life. So, I called the Earthlink's 800-number. Remember back to the good old days at the beginning of the year when we were prompted to press various numbers if we wanted to speak to certain departments?

Just when some of us have figured out how to do that, new technology comes along. We don't press numbers anymore. Now we are asked to repeat words into the telephone receiver while a computer at the other end listens to us and decides if what we're saying has merit.

"Because you are very, very important and we care about our customers, this call may be monitored for quality control. Please say the name of the department you want to speak to," a computerized voice said.

"Technical support," I said.

"Do you want customer support or technical support?" the voice asked.

"I already told you what I want," I replied.

"I'm sorry, I don't understand the word already."

"Technical support," I repeated.

"Did you say technical support?"

"Yes," I said gnashing my teeth together. "That's exactly what I said."

"I'm sorry. I don't understand the word exactly."

"I want to talk to your supervisor," I yelled into the phone.

"I can connect you with the mainframe, but you'll have to call back during normal business hours."

"It's two p.m. These are normal business hours," I whined.

"Not for a computer. Computers work between the hours of 2 and 5 a.m."

"Well, what about you? You're working now."

"I'm special."

"I'll say you're special. Can I talk to a real person?"

"I'm sorry. All of our representatives are busy helping other customers."

"Well, I'll wait."

"Your waiting time is six hours and 45 minutes. Thank you for calling Earthlink."

Two days later, I was awakened by a little girl voice.

"Hey, how're you doin'?"

"I'm having some trouble with my email."

"Bummer," said the perky voice. "Maybe you should switch to AOL."

"You're telling me to try your competitor? Aren't you afraid of being fired?" I asked.

"They won't fire me, I'm only 11 years old. No one over 13 understands how these computers work. I have two more years on my contract. Hey, do you mind if I put you on hold?"

City Different Technology

I was thumbing through computer magazines the other day because I like keeping up in case I move some place that has electricity that doesn't blink on and off every few minutes.

The latest buzzwords are smart phones, Wi-Fi, flash memory and something called the Tablet PC, which may or may not plug into your PDA, MP3, DVD-RW/CD-RW or portable printer, because although the technology may be new, it doesn't necessarily work any better than anything else.

We save a lot of money on high tech gadgets by living in Santa Fe.

Take the telephone situation, for example. The average home in Santa Fe does not have access to DSL lines, the high-speed Internet access telephone service.

That's because there's something wrong with our telephone lines. They're old and have holes in them or something that doesn't permit them to carry high-speed data.

This is unless you live on the expensive East Side, which does have DSL access; or the West Side, which barely has any kind of telephone service, but has a lot of speed bumps.

If you live in the county like me, you're just happy to get the road graded occasionally.

Now, all this brings me back to how we save money by living here. Since there is nothing to plug these new gadgets into, there's no sense in buying them in the first place.

After all, who needs a smart phone with all the bells and whistles when you don't have the bells and whistles, which, by the way, are sold separately and work on an operating system that does not work with your particular computer.

The newest gadget is the Tablet PC. It's bigger than a PDA, such as the iPaq, which no matter what our President may think is nowhere near Iraq.

The Tablet PC may or may not have a keyboard, but it plugs into your PDA, which plugs into your desktop computer, which plugs into your MP3 player permitting you to play soothing music while trying to figure out if your phone is so smart, why doesn't it work when it rains.

Let's face it, technology has not only taken over our lives, but we are running out of places to plug it all into.

Just the other day, I was driving along Rodeo Road when I accidentally plugged my radar detector into my MP3 player and heard Police Chief Bev Lennon's voice over my car radio warning me to slow down or else she'd install speed bumps in my driveway.

The good news is that just as we are running out of plugs, someone has invented Wi-Fi, which is communication without cables, wires or plugs.

The bad news is that we all know things that work in other places don't work in Santa Fe.

Daytime TV Bad for Health

There it was, the headline of my nightmares. "Daytime TV weakens immune system of Santa Fe woman."

I discovered this truth while ripping through the TV guide with the hunger a gourmand usually reserves for tracking down a good meal.

I blame my own sudden good taste on a lingering cold that made child's play of the cardinal rule that a cold lasts seven days if you see a doctor, and a week if you don't.

My cold was the worst in recorded history. After two weeks, I realized I needed professional help fast. That's when I reached for the daily TV logs.

I have a satellite dish, which means that like cable subscribers, I'm paying a lot of money to receive a lot of channels broadcasting absolutely nothing of interest to anything with a brain.

Cable pretends to give you a choice about what you watch; satellite doesn't even pretend. The main difference is that the satellite people are actually nice on the telephone, while the cable folks are usually out to lunch.

I miss watching local programming, a depravation I began suffering the minute the little dish went up on my roof.

"I'm sorry, Ms. Kusel," said the voice on the phone. "You aren't able to get signals for local programs. We don't broadcast any local channels. If you'd like, you could receive local channels from some other area."

Admittedly, the idea of watching some other town's city council duke it out on a public access channel was fleetingly attractive, but I declined.

I had declined into the kind of hypnotic stupor that accompanies fever and mistakenly grabbed a TV program guide instead of the telephone book, when I suddenly realized that the common cold is caused by daytime television programming.

Biologists traced the mutant gene to a frustrated wordsmith, who, through supernatural powers is able to boil down entire movie plots into a one-phrase synopsis.

But don't take my word for it, read it for yourself.

"Inherit the Wind." A man stands trial for teaching Darwinism.

"Powder." Pale-skinned teen has supernatural powers.

"Superman: The Movie." Reporter Clark Kent has another identity.

"Godzilla." An embattled giant lizard fights for life.

"The Kiss." Feline beauty spreads Belgian Congo voodoo in suburbia.

"Delicatessen." Future underground vs. black-market cannibal butcher.

"The Third Day." Amnesiac faces unhappy wife, rotten cousin.

"Custer of the West." General Custer offends politicians, winds up at Little Bighorn.

"Hud." Texas rancher's son acts rotten.

"The Blob." A teen rebel and a cheerleader fight formless slime oozing through town engulfing locals. (See following entry.)

"Morons from Outer Space." Dimwits from Blob crash-land and become pop stars.

Don't look now, but I think this last one is a true story. I've seen these people walking around town.

It's OK to Cry

The world cried when the first bombs fell in the Iraqi desert.

We are told not to underestimate the depth of our depression and sadness over world events, but rather to acknowledge it as a first step toward healing.

I remind myself that it is OK to cry while watching the TV war coverage.

I tell myself that tears will help keep me from becoming inured to the scars of battle.

For those of us who have lived long enough, man's inhumanity to man is not a new revelation. What does astonish is that we somehow forgot, and are again surprised.

Once we brandish the flags of God and country, we are regrettably capable of anything. But make no mistake; we are not alone in this, with both sides proclaiming the protection and guidance of the omnipotent, I wonder what's left for the rest of us.

While some of us see the war as clear and compelling, necessary for freeing a people from a tyrannical regime, others view war as an illegal and immoral rout, foisted upon a people by a powerful madness led by corporate war profiteers.

Whether pro or con, all must admit that war is obscene, a psychotic break with reality, just as peace at any price is a sophomoric wish.

Watching the war unfold on TV must necessarily touch the lives of all of us. The faces of the young men and women are the faces of youth.

They are the faces of ordinary Americans like you and me. While we pray for their return, their lives will be changed, forever robbed of their youth.

Sadly, we are witnessing the end of an America that we know and dearly love.

Just as Bush has systemically removed us from treaties that hold all humanity answerable to the rest of the world, he has instilled in us a right of preemptive action: the right to wage war before war is waged on us.

We have abandoned a role of leadership in the community of man. We have become a rogue nation in a rogue world.

Such terms as "rules of war" and "rules of engagement" are reminiscent of an acerbic poem by Stephen Crane, in which the American poet proclaims, "Do not weep, maiden, for war is kind."

Historically, Mesopotamia, which embraces Iraq, is noted as the cradle of civilization, and we can only hope it doesn't become its crypt.

Americans again are on the march. The sounds of munitions and falling bombs ricochet in our ears. We watch through tears as body bags are zipped and wrapped in our flag.

We salute who we were as Americans, while nervously awaiting who we have become.

"Do not weep, mother, for war is kind."

What They Say, What They Mean

Nothing is what it seems, and this is never more apparent than when you're trying to get something done over the phone.

What they say and what they mean are entirely different.
So here's how it works. You call and become mired in a communications swamp that quickly reduces you to babbling gibberish, usually to a computer that doesn't care about your rapidly diminishing mental state.

So, pull up a chair, pick up the telephone, press the hold button and begin repeating after me:

What they are saying: I'm sorry, you must first Dial one before completing your number.

What they mean: Because U.S. West is not making enough money in New Mexico, we will be doing everything in our power to confuse you. Although you really did Dial one, we're pretending you didn't, thereby forcing you to question your own mental state.

What they are saying: This call may be monitored for quality control.

What they mean: We are spying on some of our employees and are trying to force them into taking an early retirement.

What they are saying: Please don't hang up. One of our cheerful Customer Claims Advisers will be able to assist you in processing your medical claim.

What they mean: Just cool your jets. One of our high school dropouts will be with you just as soon as they finish talking to their friends to decide whether or not you will be given the medication your doctor has prescribed for you.

What they are saying: All of our representatives are busy helping other customers. But please don't hang up. Your call is important to us, and will be answered in the order it was received.

What they mean: If you really were important to us, we would have given you the same private number we give our friends.

What they are saying: The information you may receive is not legally binding. By staying on the line, you agree to our terms.

What they mean: Because we pay minimum wage, the operator who answers your call has not received any training and probably doesn't know what he or she is talking about anyway. So take everything they say to you with a grain of salt. They are here only because some of you refuse to talk to a machine.

What they are saying: If you are calling from a Touch Tone phone, please Press four. If you are calling from a rotary phone, please stay on the line and one of our operators will assist you.

What they mean: Everyone has Touch Tone phones, and if you don't, you probably are living in an old house, are old yourself and are therefore not interested in all the bells and whistles like caller ID that we can sell you to add on to your telephone service. You can stay on the line, but don't expect anyone to ever talk to you.

What they are saying: Thank you for calling the Psychic Hotline. Please wait for one of our highly talented psychics to come one the line to help you with your inner-most concerns and help you figure out what's going on in your life.

What they mean: Uh-oh, there's another nut from Santa Fe on the line who wants us to look into the future and tell them when the city phones will be working again.

Where Sideways Is Just Another Direction

It's not our mistake that our area code and zip code are both being changed at the same time.

It took a lot of planning to throw Santa Feans off balance. Which, of course, is not hard to do since most of us are prone to that anyway.

Come with me to a meeting at the Department of Confusion, where "Sideways is always just another direction."

At first glance, the people sitting around the table look vaguely suspicious. For one, their clothes match; even the women are wearing ties, and virtually all are wearing shoes. They're clearly not locals.

"Let's call this meeting to order. We need a new game plan. People are becoming complacent. Now that the ethnicity of museum docents has run its course, we need something new to stir up the masses," the chairperson said.

"You're right, blaming the schools for everything has grown tiresome," came a reply.

"What about changing zip codes?" the chairperson queried.

"You're kidding. People already don't get their mail. Changing the zip codes would be bedlam. How soon can we do it?"

"Well, first, we'll have to devise a way to make people think about something else, like area codes. People are in love with their cell phones, and the thought of missing out on a call causes them to become antsy," the chairperson said.

"I think I see what you're talking about, but only fools would change two things at once."

"Yes, exactly. We'll just say the changes will benefit the average person."

"How will mixing up telephone calls and the mail service all at once benefit anyone?" someone wondered aloud.

"Let's face it, a lot of us end up with our neighbor's mail, while others have so many phone numbers the thought of remembering them all is impossible. We'll tell people change is good. And just to show we haven't lost our sense of humor, we'll throw in a new P.I.N., which they'll have to memorize," the chairperson offered.

"What's the P.I.N. for?"

"Nothing specific, we just thought it would be a good thing for the future."

"Don't you think we should try this out in the rural areas first?"

"That's not any fun. The population is too small. We need something that will affect the most people. We'll tell them we have a new game for them to play. We can tie it in with gambling."

"You mean like choosing a favorite number?"

"We'll say it's a crapshoot if they get their mail at all, and the luck of the draw as to what area code they end up with."

4

LIVING IN SANTA FE

Surviving the Plaza

Tell me, Mr. Un-Mayor, what is it going to take to stop traffic around the Plaza?

How many pedestrians have to be hit, dragged and maimed on our downtown streets before something is done to alleviate a dangerous situation?

It isn't as if this were a new problem. This column has been calling for banning traffic on Santa Fe's historic center ever since its inception more than four years ago.

Before that, there were citizens' groups, Letters to the Editor of this newspaper and a stunned populace after a young boy who "borrowed" his dad's car drove it out of control and crashed into the Palace of Governors.

This time a motorist with a long string of DWI arrests hit and dragged two victims, one of who is in an Albuquerque hospital hanging on to life by a thread.

These were tourists, Mr. Un-Mayor, and if nothing else, tourist dollars talk and are heard in Santa Fe.

It is time for you to actually do something. But moving into action is not your way, so you've decided to appoint a task force to, uh, study the situation.

What needs to be studied? Ban the traffic. Make the Plaza safe for people. Let me save you a little time and agonizing over a decision. Put up the barriers. Reroute the cars.

The mayor and City Council must put aside differences and move at once.

There simply is not room for pedestrians and automobiles on the narrow streets immediately bordering Santa Fe's historic district.

Let it be known that the City of Santa Fe has made a decision to close the Plaza to traffic because we value life.

Remember, this is not a new problem. It's not as if the city's governing body has never had to think of closing the Plaza before.

It has been a festering thorn in our sides for years. We can't close our eyes to today's problems and blame it on history anymore than the mayors and governing bodies in such cities as London, Verona and towns in Mexico did when they took steps to close their zocolos to traffic.

We also must ask where are our Downtown business leaders? Why aren't they demanding street closure?

What about the American Indians who sell their wares beneath the portals of one of this nation's oldest public buildings? They must take a stand for protecting their own health against automobile fumes.

Meanwhile, the city is "studying" the situation and appointing still another task force, further distancing itself from direct responsibility.

Today, we are shocked. We are saddened and we demand action. We are Santa Fe and we all are culpable for what happens on our streets.

The Plaza needs this community in order to survive. But first we have to survive the Plaza.

Going Nowhere in the Rail Yard

It's time to kick some butt. It's time for the people to take the rail yard into our own hands. Set up some tents, stake out the area as our own—which it is—and crack the whip.

If city government isn't capable of dealing with the rail yard, we are.

If after reading Ellen Berkovich's stories in "Pasatiempo," on how the City of Albuquerque took the bull by the horns and infused its malingering downtown with a vibrant blend of art and life didn't make you grind your teeth, you need to read it again.

We're talking about Albuquerque here, folks. When Albuquerque begins sounding more interesting than Santa Fe, we had better sit up and take notice.

The place always has been our biggest joke to the south. Now, thanks to our City Council dragging its collective feet on the rail yard, the joke's on us. But for once, I lost my sense of humor.

I'm frustrated. I'm frustrated because we are paying for the rail yard and it's expensive enough to live here without sitting quietly throwing good money after bad.

My message to the City Council is this: If you can't do the job, quit. Move aside. Get out of town. As Albuquerque Mayor Jim Baca succinctly said in Ellen Berkovich's article: "Get out of the way, and let us fix this city."

Albuquerque has managed to come up with a hefty mix of private and public space usage, back-to-back. It didn't happen overnight, but neither did the rail yard fiasco.

For the last decade we've watched it sit like an open sore, festering with trash right before our eyes, a testament to the ineptitude of the leadership in this city.

If you think the average person can't make a difference, look at what two mothers did when they bemoaned the fact that their small children didn't have a place to go in this city.

They built the Santa Fe Children's Museum. Vibrant from the start, and now entering its 13th year. Perhaps we could convince Ellen Biderman and Ellyn Feldman—the two Ellens, who kick-started the children's museum on a chunk of state property adjacent to Plan B—into heading up the rail yard development.

Perhaps we could convince Frieda Arth, who has more energy than any 10 people I know, to complete the triumvirate.

She doesn't have a political axe to grind. She's already had a successful career and now donates her experience to non-profits because she believes things can get done by interested, caring people.

Perhaps they could do what the city could not—get things moving without the albatross of politics hanging around their necks.

They're not strangers about asking for money to fund a project for the common good.

If you think that this city council's approval of cookie-cutter box store after box store on Cerrillos Road represents progress, then look again; we are rapidly turning into Albuquerque. But the old Albuquerque, the one without leadership. And this grieves me greatly.

What happened to our dream of this lively place that reflected the interesting ways of the people who lived and worked in the area?

What happened, indeed?

"What happens to a dream deferred?" asked 20th Century poet Langston Hughes. "It stinks like rotten meat."

In the meantime, does anyone have a tent I could borrow?

The Matter of the Shoes

It's about the sign affixed to a cardboard box on the corner of Old Pecos Trail near Calle Medico.

Never mind that the county hadn't even gotten around to sanding the roads leading into town, and forget about having to use a match to thaw out the keyhole in the car door; someone had been there.

On the first snowstorm of the season, the one we've all been praying for, someone had been out in the dead of night to put up a sign reading, "What's with the shoes?"

Shoes have been appearing around that same spot for more than a decade. The intersection suffered a strange makeover when the highway was revamped and a large island removed back when Debbie Jaramillo was the acalde, but that didn't stop the shoes. They were simply adjusted for wear and moved three feet north.

It might be the corner itself. Imagine spending millions to install crosswalks and a traffic signal where no one ever crosses; a place where the arrow has been frozen into a permanent, green grimace pointing toward the Plaza.

Careful watchers of the cityscape should have known something was afoot. It always happens around the time marking the changing of a season; like a secret sign from outer space, pulses quicken, a ring appears around the moon and shoes begin marching onto the island.

It's usually one shoe. On rare occasions, a pair has been sighted.

Last week, a right ski boot lined with faux fleece was abandoned on its side for nearly a week.

It's one of those urban myths. All of a sudden, shoes starting appearing there and people initiated conversations. Strangers began sharing information, giving each other soleful winks and nods.

It was a community event even Santa Feans could agree on. A sense of civic pride that didn't raise taxes and proffer empty political promises.

I have a shoe rescued from that very corner from New Year's Eve, 1992. A barely worn, silver, lame sling back. Size 12.

Through the years, I have fantasized about the owner. If it belonged to a woman, she must have been the size of Barbarella. If it belonged to a drag queen, she was probably on her way to a great party with a matching feather boa and fake eyelashes long enough to dust her painted toes.

The shoe joined my collection of one other; that one from Maria Benitez, which I did not find in the road, but was given to me so I would stop pestering her to let me join her flamenco troupe.

Through the years, there have been Birkenstocks, sports shoes with colorful soles, children's oxfords, work boots and one, basic black pump no doubt tossed by someone casting away a prior identity as a state office worker.

Hey, Roswell, keep your space museum, Santa Fe's steppin' out.

The Sidewalk Payoff

After our wet winter, Barbara noticed the sidewalks in front of her house had been damaged by repeated thawing and freezing, so she called the city to see what to do about repairs.

Barbara, which is not her real name, said she spoke to Antonio Trujillo at the Department of Public Works. He told her he would send an inspector.

A few days later, she received a visit from a city inspector, whom we'll call Mike. She said Mike drove up in a city truck, looked at the sidewalk and told her that she indeed needed to repair walkway.

"The red flag went up when he told me he could do the work himself," Barbara said. "He also gave me the names of three other contractors he said worked on sidewalks."

Being a wily consumer, Barbara called the other companies.

"Two told me they didn't do sidewalks, and the third didn't exist," she said.

That's when she went to the Yellow Pages. She found the name of a contractor with a valid New Mexico license, and then called the Better Business Bureau to check out the company's track record.

A few weeks later, Mike stopped by again, and once again, he was driving a city truck. Barbara told him she was thinking of going with another contractor and was waiting for a bid.

"He told me to contact him when I got the other bid because he could under-cut the other guy," Barbara said. "He also told me he wouldn't charge me tax."

She asked Mike for a bid in writing. She never got it. She also asked him for a business card. She never got that, either.

A few days later, she received a call from Mike asking her if she had made up her mind.

She had. She was going with the other contractor.

"He asked me the contractor's name so he could check his files to see if he was listed," Barbara said. "Mike called back and told me that the other contractor was not listed. He warned me that the other contractor would need to post a $10,000 surety bond."

That's when Barbara called me. And that's when I called Antonio Trujillo to ask him a few questions of my own.

"We don't fix sidewalks unless the city is the owner of the abutting property," Trujillo told me. "We usually just send an inspector."

What about city employees moonlighting the work themselves?

"When people ask for names, I tell them to look in the Yellow Pages," Trujillo said.

"I know things are done differently here in Santa Fe, but is this how business is conducted?" she asked.

Well, Barbara, not exactly.

Highway to Nowhere

I once worked with a printer at *The New Mexican* named Gene Goodman.

Gene, who is now retired, had one of those personalities that didn't suffer fools easily. I, of course, was one of those fools.

Many was the night we stood in the composing room locking horns over page layout.

Now, I'll tell you a little secret. When an editor (me) asks the printer (him) to change something, it usually gets changed. But not with Gene. I once asked him to change something, and Gene looked up at me and said, "Not at this newspaper."

And that was that. For some odd reason, Gene and I have remained friends and when I ran into him recently, he reminded me of The Curious Case of the North/South Signs on Route 466.

It seems State Road 466 runs on St. Michaels Drive from its northwest end at Cerrillos Road (or Highway 14) to its southwest juncture with the Old Pecos Trail, and then southwest along the Old Pecos Trail to its other end near I-25.

Gene pointed out there are approximately six signs along St. Mikes identifying it as SR 466. The most recent official state highway map identifies it this way, too.

Now, this is where it gets dicey. The map published by the Auto Club identifies the entire St. Michaels-Old Pecos Trail route as 466, but mistakenly acknowledges Old Pecos Trail as "Las Vegas Highway."

Three of the 466 highway signs are designated North or South directions.

The first directional sign, located at the southerly end of the highway, between the traffic signals at the corner of Old Las Vegas Highway/Rodeo Road and Santa Barbara Road. You can see it while driving in a northwesterly direction. The sign says you are driving "South."

The second sign is on St. Mikes approaching St. Vincent Hospital driving toward the Jemez. You're headed northwest, but the sign says, "South."

Gene mentioned this to a couple of women who live out Old Las Vegas Highway. They told him the situation was OK for locals who understand things like this, but it might be tough on tourists.

He next contacted traffic engineer David Roybal, who acknowledged that a similar anomaly existed on northbound I-25 going toward Colorado when the highway actually heads south for a number of miles.

Then Gene called Matias Montoya in the state's cartography department.

Together they figured that what is now SR 466 used to be Business I-25.

The wrong North-South designations were a holdover from the days when you went north on Old Pecos Trail in order to go south to Albuquerque.

I don't know about you, but for me, this certainly explains everything.

Florida's Got Nothin' on New Mexico

The truth needs to be told. I may have just gotten back after visiting Fidel's Cuba, but that wasn't the real reason I left Santa Fe.

I really flew down to Miami to help with the election results.

The officials down there needed someone with a strong understanding of how real voting stuff works, which is why someone from Santa Fe was called in.

Of course, I was surprised as you are now when I received the phone call asking if I could drop everything I was doing in Santa Fe and rush out to Miami.

True, I was planning a road trip to the Alien Museum in Roswell, but I soon was convinced to drop that. After all, the voice on the phone said, what could be stranger than the national election goings on.

"The truth is out there, Denise," the voice said on the phone. "And we need your help."

"Well, I was going to go to Albertson's for groceries, but I could fly to Miami," I said with a flourish. "But how can I help you?"

"It's your experience as a New Mexican during the election process that we're looking for," he said.

"I have a lot of experience in voting here," I agreed. "After all, I remembered to get to the firehouse to cast my ballot before the machines broke down five minutes after the polls opened, didn't I? "

I paused for a moment to collect my thoughts. I thought it best to level with these folks before I agreed to help.

"Listen, I have to warn you, I live in Santa Fe County, not up there in Rio Arriba, where they've turned voting into an art form."

"We know that, but the phones aren't working up there since the telephone company decided they're not making enough money in New Mexico. They may have changed their name, but not their tune," he took a breath, and then added, "Now we understand that in Northern New Mexico, the dead can vote."

"Yes, that's true," I said. "It's a little known law but one the politicos rely on."

"This sounds like the forward thinking we need here in Florida," he said. "How did this come about?"

"Well, as you know, in order to qualify for electoral votes, a process we don't understand anyway, we had to have enough people registered at the polls. It was believed that by allowing the dead to vote, we could get that badly needed extra electoral vote."

"How did you keep people from catching on? I mean, wouldn't someone recognize the fact that the same names were being used over and over again?"

"Well, that's true, Ed. May I call you Ed?" I asked picking up a clue from talk radio where sincere friendships are created in an instant.

"My name is Bill, but you can call me Ed."

"Good, I like someone who is not afraid of change. A lot of the names are used more than once because there are a lot of people here who have the same names. Santa Fe is an old town and it just goes to figure that we would run out of new names before long. That's why we use the old ones again."

"Oh, I get it. It's sort of recycling," he breathed into the receiver.

"I suppose you could call it that. But due to past life regression, we are allowed to vote more than once. It's a county ordinance."

"How soon can you get out here?" he asked.

Firing up for Summer

Only fools and the City Council have just realized that Santa Fe is in a desperate fire situation this summer because of a prolonged drought.

Some of us have already begun landscaping with drought-tolerant native plants. Others got the message before the smoke from the 2000 Cerro Grande fire cleared.

While our City Council finally began wondering where all the water to sustain growth is coming from, we're using buckets to collect shower water for our plants and praying we don't have the combination of a windy day and a wildfire.

We asked Claudia Standish, a Wildland Urban Interface Specialist for the Santa Fe National Forest, for some realistic tips about what average folks like you and me can do to help guard our homes against wildfires.

Part of Standish's job is to work with homeowners to help them make informed decisions and give them tools to assess their property and create what she calls "a firewise landscape."

"It took the Cerro Grande to really drive it home that it just isn't in California where houses burn up in wildfires," Standish said. "It's about as bad or maybe worse than 2000 (the Cerro Gordo fire). The fires in Riudoso and Cloudcroft already have told us a lot.

"This year's fire behavior is more severe because there's so much fuel out there," Standish reminded. "The western ecosystem is designed this way. The only thing we can do is try to live in that system and make solid decisions on how we're going to live here.

"I hear people asking what the government is going to do," she said. "Let me tell you how it really is: We can help you see what it is we see, but you have to learn to view your landscape with new eyes.

"Everybody has to get together and work. Fires don't care about fences. The best policy is for people to empower themselves by developing neighborhood clusters."

But just as drought doesn't suddenly happen, working to clean up yards and rake pine needles is a process that takes time.

By working together little by little with your neighbors, it can be done. Using the same concept as a neighborhood watch, set up a committee and then call Standish at 438-7805 to make an appointment for her to come out and talk.

If you can't handle the raking and cleaning by yourself, hire young people. Kids are looking for jobs. Hire them to help you rake pine needles and get the trash ready to haul to the dump. But remember to pay them.

They may be young, but they have expenses and dignity, too.

In fact, I am challenging the Santa Fe City Council to set up a hometown version of the Civil Conservation Corps, paying teenagers to help make Santa Fe firewise.

A Secret Meeting of Health Officials

Take heart, fellow New Mexicans, federal health officials issued a smallpox preparedness plan instructing states to get ready to vaccinate every American in the event of a biological attack using smallpox. The plan calls for inoculating as many as one million people in 10 days.

But can we really expect this in a state that can't even get it together to dispense an annual flu vaccine?

Every year, while other states are practically giving away flu shots, New Mexicans go wanting as officials fall back on the excuse that they were caught off guard.

This happens because officials were not expecting another October, which is the beginning of flu season.

So let's listen in on a hypothetical secret meeting of state health officials as they discuss the options.

Health Secretary: "I don't know what you guys are worried about; we had an October last year, but this doesn't mean we're going to have another one."

Official #1: "What is he talking about?"

Official #2: "Well, it's true, we did have an October last year. You can't fault him for not telling the truth."

Official #1: "But what about this year? It's a whole new ballpark."

Health Secretary: "Hey, whatever happened to that ballpark Albuquerque was renovating?"

Official #2: "Someone made a mistake and went too far, so it had to be completely rebuilt."

Health Secretary: "What was left?"

Official #2: "Third base. But what about flu shots?"

Official #1: "Do we need them yet?"

Official #2 "No, the yearly epidemic hasn't started."

Official #1: "Relax, we'll just tell people to eat a lot of chile and they'll be safe."

Health Secretary: " Chile? Red or green?"

Official #1: "Does it make a difference?"

Official #2: "It does to New Mexicans."

Health Secretary: "Let's push green chile as a flu vaccine. We'll say, 'Eat green before you turn green.' "

Official #1: "What about the smallpox scare? There's no way we'll be ready to dispense smallpox inoculations before 2010."

Health Secretary: "How come?"

Official #2: "Because New Mexico doesn't have enough health care professionals. We don't pay them anything, so they leave."

Health Secretary: "Ingrates. We'll use the chile idea for smallpox, too. This time, we'll say red chile is a smallpox preventive."

Official #1 "It might work. Red looks good in the bag. Besides, we can ship it to Arizona."

Official #2: "Don't they have their own chile?"

Health Secretary: " Arizona doesn't even know how to tax food, like we do."

Official #1: "Listen, we need a catchy phrase that people can remember."

Health Secretary: "What about, 'Better red than dead.' "

Puppies of Mass Destruction

Springtime in Santa Fe is when people come out of hibernation and we see folks we haven't seen for four months perusing the plants at the nursery.

Anything is possible. Even the rocks in my yard are bursting with potential. Well, not really. Not even close.

I have grasped reality. Looked it in the face. Wiped tears from my eyes and admitted that nothing will grow in my yard.

I've tried everything: Yum-Yum mix. That other stuff in a jar that everyone swears by. Even the plants at Santa Fe Greenhouses have a tag that says, "Will grow in direct sunlight to 50 feet with no water. Except at Denise's house, where it will grow to a height of minus five inches."

This is why I don't actually buy anything at the nursery. I just go there for the social value: To schmooze and give advice, helping people decide what to plant since I have long experience with every plant there.

"Yes, this one should grow very nice in a container. These will look lovely in a small garden. This is very drought tolerant. Great for Santa Fe."

The nursery should give me a company shirt for all the time I've spent there examining the potentials of grow- anywhere-in-the-world wild flower seeds and soil amenders.

But first you need soil to amend. I have even loosed my Puppies of Mass Destruction into the yard and ordered them to dig.

Not as easy as it sounds. I had to wake the basset from a sound sleep and get him off the chair, which is where he spends his days.

Nights, of course, he transfers his dreams to my bed, where he sleeps crossways, managing to take up the entire bed with both ears and a tail.

I urged him out into the yard with the promise of cookies. Once there, he acted as if I were crazy and immediately jumped up on his outside couch for a nap.

He's right. I am crazy. There is no soil to dig his feet into.

Paddy the bearded collie doesn't dig. He wasn't bred to dig. He guards. He stands there watching me hauling soil from the compost pile; caring for it as if it were gold instead of converted garbage, and placing it lovingly into what's left of last year's flowerbeds.

Within two minutes even the worms are racing back to the compost pile. Something in their evolution has told them you can't make enriched soil from rock.

Yoda the corgi refuses to come out of the house. She's busy watching her food bowl in case something from outer space should suddenly drop into it.

Only Callie the Santa Fe River dog is happy. He's deaf and nearly blind. His tail is always wagging. In his mind there are flowers. Even in winter. Even in my yard.

The Santa Fe Stink

I was calling out for lunch, but then somehow the telephone lines got crossed and instead of the pizza guy, I tapped into a conversation at City Hall.

City Councilor: "Is this a secure line?"

Un-Mayor: "We don't have secure lines in Santa Fe. We barely have telephone service. What's on your mind?"

City Councilor: "Well, I've been thinking of ways to get peoples' minds off their water bills."

Un-Mayor: "They don't have their minds on their water bills. We haven't sent any out in six months."

City Councilor: "I mean when we finally send the rest of them

146

out. Our only hope is confusion. We'll say we've forgotten to send out sewer bills, too. That way, no one will know exactly what to complain about when they call."

Un-Mayor: "They'll never believe we neglected sewer bills, too."

City Councilor: "We can drive the point home by inventing something sewer-related. We'll call it the Agua Fria Stench."

Un-Mayor: "I like that. It rolls off your tongue easily. But what is it?"

City Councilor: "Well, we don't know what it is. All we know is that it smells bad."

Un-Mayor: "I don't know about this. People usually don't believe things they can't see."

City Councilor: "What about the Taos Hum? Half the town of Taos is looking for the hum."

Un-Mayor: "Yeah, but that's Taos. They'll do anything for entertainment. Besides the hum is good for tourism. Who in their right mind would come to Santa Fe for the Agua Fria Stench besides people from Taos? They'll think it's because we have a water shortage we can't bathe."

City Councilor: "Well, we need something to get the peoples' minds off the fact that we don't know what we're doing. We need someone to blame. We need the ultimate smoke screen. What about the Rail Yard?"

Un-Mayor: "I told you to never mention the Rail Yard around me. It makes me see red. Now, what about it?"

City Councilor: "Let's ditch it."

Un-Mayor: "We can't do that. It's too big to just forget. Besides we owe money on the property."

City Councilor: "I know that, but it's not like we've actually done anything with it. Maybe we need to put someone else in charge so we have someone to blame about nothing getting done."

Un-Mayor: "Blame? I like that. It's beginning to sound promising.

First, we get the people confused with the water and sewer bills not being sent out, and then we tell them we have to hire someone else to handle the Rail Yard. But who do we blame it on?"

City Councilor: "The city manager."

Un-Mayor: "Which one? I can't keep track. It's getting so you can't tell the players without a program."

City Councilor: "Hey, what's that noise?"

Un-Mayor: "I was just humming. But what's that stench?"

City Councilor: "I was just thinking."

People's Park

It isn't so much a park as it is a vacant lot. But it really doesn't matter what it's called because until recently the only things that ever went down in it were drug deals and drinking.

It was the kind of place parents told their kids to stay away from and old women with shopping bags gave it a wide detour.

"So, whose park is this?" I ask.

A bunch of kids who are sitting around a metal picnic table begin to laugh. Everything about them says kids except their eyes. Their eyes are weary with life.

"Whose park? That's a good question," says 19-year-old Andres Gallegos. A smile forms on his face, but quickly disappears. "No one really wants to take responsibility for it."

In 1986, the city was fat with tourist dollars and pumped some money into putting in a sand pile with some play equipment. But in the way of such things, the equipment fell into disrepair before finally disappearing altogether.

148

Word on the street is that someone from the city came over on a Sunday morning and took it away. What's left is a single swing and a set of metal rings.

Andres is one of a cadre of youth who are working to squeeze some life back into the park through a mural project called Little Ghetto Love, which is funded by the city through a grant to the Life Center for Youth and Development.

Today, Andres sits on a ledge with a bunch of other kids. Waiting for something to happen. It's hot in the relentless way of a late August afternoon, so he sucks on a Coke, slowly turning the plastic container around in his hands.

If this were on Santa Fe's Eastside, it would be called a postage stamp park, denoting its size. But this isn't the Eastside, and unless you know where to look, this neighborhood is invisible.

Located in a small slice of a subsidized housing project called 2nd Street La Canada, the park nests on Mann Avenue, between Second and Fifth streets.

As for the park, well, for one thing, there's no shade; for another, two loaded dumpsters face the street. They stink of summer. It's that sweet, ripe smell, like cantaloupe that's been around too long. In fact, once you smell it, you spend the next 15 minutes trying to tell your nose to forget it.

"Oh, man, that's gross," I say, trying to bury myself in my notebook.

No one answers. This isn't something new. They're used to it. This is their neighborhood. A few feet away, shards of broken glass glitter in the children's sandbox, like so many lost diamonds in this vacant lot of forgotten ownership.

Artist Shelley Horton-Trippe, who has been active on the Santa Fe art scene since the mid-1970s, which happens to be before all of these kids were born, heads up the mural project.

She raised her own children in Santa Fe on whatever money she could make selling her work and doing public art projects.

Her idea here was to put some locals to work, teaching them skills plus a chance to work on a socially relevant piece of public art.

The project eventually employed eight paid youth between 15 and 23. Add to this, the 15 or so little kids who sometimes showed up and you have a crew.

"We had a three-year-old, who was painting. If they came and said they wanted to paint, we gave them a brush. These youth are creating pride and a sense of ownership of their neighborhood," Shelley says.

She also worked with such Santa Fe businesses as Wellborn Paint, Blue Sky Soda, Mesa Steel Inc. and Denman & Associates, all of which donated money or products.

Shelley is talking while standing beneath a *sombra*, a permanent shade structure donated by Denman & Associates. But it isn't working at the moment. The sun is blasting in from the west, swallowing the shade.

Shelley gives her bottle of Coke a shake and watches as the brown fizz works its way to the top.

An Izuzu Trooper pulls up and Jesus "Chuey" Gonzales climbs down. Chuey is new to mural painting. Before this, the biggest design he ever drew was sketched on a *panio*, handkerchief art created by guys doing time in prison. But now he's working in a large scale. He's created two distinct murals on the two sides of the Dumpster enclosure that can be seen.

On one side, Chuey has drawn a picture of a mother and father lovingly holding a baby. The father in the drawing wears Chuey's face, right down to the tear tattooed on the corner of his left eye.

On the other side, Chuey has created an image of a Hispanic man in the prime of his life, breaking free from chains and emerging from the flames of his past life with his arms outstretched.

Here in this park where the only colors are those on discarded candy wrappers, brightly colored pink and orange roses painted by Cristina Griego, 15, surround the image.

150

They call Andres the car expert. His part of the project is painting a series of low riders along a low reach of wall at the back of Little Ghetto Love.

"There's going to be the front of a '57 Chevy over here," he says, pointing with his chin. "Over there, I think it'll be a Pan Am."

But right now, he's just sitting on a metal picnic table in this oppressive heat. Andres squints into the sun, blasted by a hot wind. He watches Jesse Williams approaching from the street. The wind tugs at her blonde hair.

Jesse is an AmeriCorps volunteer who has spent the better part of a year working in the neighborhood.

At the end of her tour, she'll go home to Atlanta and then to college in Massachusetts.

At the end of the summer, Andres Gallegos will still be here wondering how tomorrow will play out. But right now, he's listening to Jesse's ideas. In fact, he wants her job. But first, he has to get his GED, and then maybe he can get a part-time gig with AmeriCorps.

Jesse is trying to help him. They may come from different parts of the country, but they speak the same language—the language of hope.

Andres is asking about when the new computers will arrive for the community hall built by AmeriCorps volunteers. It looks like a one-room schoolhouse plopped down at the edge of the projects.

This is the place Andres will go to study for his GED, now that he has a reason to want it.

But just now, it's too hot. The wind has shifted, and I can smell the Dumpster again, but this time I don't say anything.

It's about 5:30 in the afternoon. People are getting home from work. Cars cruise by slowly, their tires crunching the gravel.

A young boy walks up with a pump water gun, pumps the action a few times and lets loose with a stream of water, drenching everyone within range. No one complains. It's welcome relief on an afternoon that feels as if someone left the oven door open.

"We get a lot of people from the community over here," Shelley says. I notice she's the only one who calls it a community. Mostly, it's not called anything at all.

"Parents come over here at night with their children. They want to see how we're doing on the mural. They want to be able to use this park again instead of being afraid of it.

"Sometimes you can see three generations living in this neighborhood," Shelley continues. "This is not just a public housing project, it's a community. The other day, this grandmother stopped by and said, `God Bless you. And thank you for doing this.' She began walking and then turned and said, `Poor people have to live somewhere, too.' "

She's right, too. There's no better way to break down the false barriers of us and them then to help teach usefulness and dignity.

In Little Ghetto Love, the two go hand-in-hand.

Kudzu Kween Strikes Again

At the grocery store, someone had the chutzpah to ask me how my garden was doing this summer.

"Very well," I lied.

"I'm so glad," he said, adjusting a grocery bag, which he had smartly constructed from a used Yum-Yum Mix sack. "You used to have so much trouble. Why, I remember the year you tried to grow kudzu and failed."

Reminded of past failures drove me to the herb aisle for a bottle of St. John's Wort.

Plants don't like me. I know that. I deal with it until mid-March, when the seed catalogues come in the mail and the rest of Santa Fe begins planting microscopic tomato seeds that eventually grow into the ones you see in Ripley's "Believe It or Nada."

We've seen these people. In late summer, they walk around town with a saltshaker and fresh tomato seeds dripping down their shirtfronts.

This year, I am trying container gardening using found objects. I especially like that cute little lard container I fashioned into a pot for morning glories. That's right, lard. Why not? I've been wearing it for years.

There's also that smart little olive tin I hauled back from Spain. There's nothing in it yet, which is why I had to make a trip to the nursery.

I'm not exactly a stranger at Santa Fe Greenhouses. Through the years, I've bought enough plants to start an entire botanical garden.

"Denise, what in the world are you doing here," smirked a clerk roaming through the perennials.

"Huh, you talking to me?" I asked casually.

"You're Denise, right? The Kudzu Kween of Santa Fe?"

"That's former Kudzu Kween. I'm into container gardening this year."

"Have you seen these?" he buzzed. "They grow very well. Sun. Shade. They thrive no matter what."

I took a six-pack of yellow flowers.

"Look here," he chirped. "These plants grow wild. They're not even picky about what kind of soil you push them into."

I put a bunch of pots filled with these purple thingies into my wagon. I just love how the nurseries give you these red wagons to schlep around. They want you to feel just like a kid again—someone with an actual future.

At my age, I don't buy saplings. I insist on fully-grown trees promising instant shade.

Once inside the car with my plants placed lovingly on the back seat, I slid the gearshift into first and began humming. That was until I looked into the rear-view mirror and saw the plants deadheading themselves, committing suicide before my eyes.

I stopped for a six-pack of cheap beer. Once home, I cracked open a couple of cold ones, put my feet up.

After all, if my life is turning into organic mulch, I might as well enjoy it.

The Street That Chases Its Own Tail

"Is this you?" the voice said on the phone.

"I don't know if it's me," I answered.

"It sounds like you. This is Ken Johnson. I just wanted to know if now that you've solved the question of going south in order to go north on I-25, what you're going to do about West Houghton?"

Now this was a question. What was I going to do about West Houghton? I hadn't considered it because I didn't know anything needed to be done.

"What's wrong with West Houghton?" I asked meekly.

"Which West Houghton are you talking about?"

"The same one you're talking about," I answered.

I used to work with Ken at The New Mexican. He was in circulation and made enough money in the stock market to retire. Not me. I'm still puttin' in the eight, so I thought I'd listen to what he had to say.

"West Houghton is a one-way loop that connects with itself at the intersection of West Houghton and West Houghton. You automatically brake at each intersection, thinking it's another four-way stop, but it isn't. It's just West Houghton."

It's the kind of street knowledge only people who deliver the newspaper and the mail know. But I did what any curious person who had nothing else in the world to do, I drove to the South Capital area to find West Houghton.

There it was, at the end of West Houghton and West Houghton. One of those Santa Fe loops a lot of us get caught in now and then.

It's those retired people who have nothing to do except make life tough for the rest of us.

Take Johnny Ray Smith, who retired from the Highway Department a while back.

"Someone was giving me directions and said, 'Turn up at the second street, and turn down at the first stop sign.' What exactly does turn up and turn down mean?" Johnny asked.

"Well, you're the one who worked for the Highway Department all those years, you tell me," I replied.

He didn't even pause to give me one of those looks people wear when they're feeling especially smug. He just launched into the answer.

"Turning up is when you turn right; turning down means you're turning left," he said.

"How do you know this?" I wondered aloud.

"It has to do with the turn signals," Johnny said. "When you turn right you toggle the lever up. Turn left, and you're pushing it down."

"C'mon, Johnny, no one uses turn signals," I reminded him.

"Well, they used to," he said innocently.

Sure, and they used to stop at red lights, too.

Welcome to Wackenhut

Roll 'em. Roll 'em. Keep those bad guys rollin' Lock 'em up. Pack 'em in. Push 'em out. Lock 'em up.

Howdy there buckaroos. Just pull that hay bale closer and hunker down. It's us, your friendly partners from the Cornell-Wackenhut Corral, just bustin' out with a new tune, "Closum Prison Blues."

It's all about that big ol' empty Main Facility out there by the County Detention Center.

Some folks see shame when they think about the old Pen. Heck, we see cash cows roamin' the prairie.

Too bad all that space is just settin' there collecting dust. We could pack 'em in. Stretch 'em out. Lock 'em down.

Partner, we're talkin' jobs here. Well, not exactly high-payin', but jobs all the same. We know how you guys in Santa Fe are chompin' at the bit for work.

Shoot, you might just say we've got you over the barrel here. The pork barrel.

Rein in that pony closer and let me tell you the story of this ill-fated prison whose name is right down there in the annals of penal fortitude, right along with Attica.

Near as we can figure, it was built for about 850 varmints. Why back in '80, business was real good. About 1,130 called it home. 'Course things got a little testy and when the smoke cleared about 33 hombres went out the door feet first.

But let's let bygones be bygones. We at Cornell want to build a better mousetrap. Spruce the old place up a little. Have dorm rooms, just like college.

Heck, we're lookin' to get 1,900 inmates inside them walls. It's all about the bottom line. We're not exactly in it for the altruistic value.

Besides, Cornell already has a track record in prison work at the County Detention Center.

Sure our employees have been complaining that they are under-trained, under-paid and under stress. But we're talkin' new 250 jobs with a $7.5 million annual grubstake.

Lemme do some 'rithmatic here. That's an average of $30,000 per person. Well, maybe not every guard is going to be making that. Just consider it another low-paying service industry, Santa Fe.

Now we're only talking about housing low-risk prisoners. Hell, they won't even be citizens.

"Non-citizen offenders awaiting deportation for relatively minor felonies…most drug-related."

That's what Cornell vice president Gary Henman said.

Not citizens? Shoot, we won't even have to worry about them writin' their congressmen. We're not talking major human rights here.

Well, sure these low-risk prisoners could, say, try to break out. But that's not the point, my friends. This is about big bucks. Why, even the old General Store is run by Cornell.

If prisoners need essentials, like a T-shirt or underwear, razors, cigarettes, soap, toothpaste, no need to have the family bring them in.

In fact, they can't. Prisoners need to buy 'em all from Cornell. This is all part of the profit picture.

So step right up, folks, it'll be standin' room only. We'll be applyin' for the contract with the federal Bureau of Prisons lickety-split. Workin' 'round the clock, we could button things up in say 90 days.

Now, never mind your Western sensibility about being herded and hog-tied. This is a gen-U-ine idea.

Sure, you just read about prisoners in the detention center sayin' they're not getting' their prescription meds. But they're the bad guys. Who're you going to believe? Just remember, folks, no prisoners, no profit.

Well, thanks for droppin' by. Real neighborly of you.

But right now it's time to round 'em up. Lock 'em down. Hold 'em in. Heck, if we could just get the guy in black to popularize the song, we'd be rollin' in dough.

The Lensic Gets a Makeover

The Lensic's Bob Martin is an idea guy.

The tip off is the way he talks about possibilities. His speech is rapid-fire. Light dances in his eyes as he drinks in the scene.

My first thought walking into the beautifully refurbished theater was that it took an energetic mind at the helm to chart a steady course.

At last, Santa Fe has a grown-up performing arts center with programming that reflects the rich pastiche of life in this town.

In the few months it's been open, more than 40 separate programs have tread the boards.

This diversity is one of the keys to its success. During the first few weeks, nine different performance groups from the public schools used the Lensic to strut their stuff across the stage, making it amply clear that this indeed was something for all Santa Feans to enjoy.

If you haven't been to the Lensic, it's worth a visit. The new look is not just window dressing. Architect Craig Hoopes did an admirable job preserving the interior of the 70-year-old theater.

Along with diversity, Martin's watchword is inclusive. That is, involve enough people, and they'll bring their friends.

"We brought a lot of (local) people along with us from the beginning," Martin said. "(A theater like this) takes a lot of work behind the scenes by people from all walks of life to make it all come together.

"I don't care if it's the Paul Taylor Dance Company or the Acequia Madre School, all groups get the same level of professionalism from us."

Martin comes to this process of thought by something he calls his "collective sensibility."

"I came of age at a time when that kind of thinking was very important," he said.

It's something he's applied to the Lensic. The values that came out of that time, such as neighborhood art and performance movements, still are viable today.

"It's something I've been doing for 20 years," Martin said. "I had to go into the community and build trust. Families are one place we sent this message. It's not us owning the event. We work together to make it happen."

Upcoming events include a locally produced variety show in the fall; a joint production between Zuni Pueblo and the Appalachian Roadside Theater in February; and the Traveling Jewish Theater in the spring.

"My goal is that every week something will be happening at the Lensic," Martin said.

If Martin is the catalyst to bring performing groups together, the community must offer support.

The Lensic is not just some place. It's our place.

They're working hard over on San Francisco Street.

And it shows.

Selling a Vacation

August is the traditional vacation month, and I suppose a number of you will be traveling to parts known and unknown.

Not me. I've decided to sell my vacation time to the City of Santa Fe. Sure, I know I don't work for the city, but if the city handles employment records the way it does everything else, no one will ever know. Which is why I found myself at City Hall the other day.

"Good morning," I said in a tone my mother would approve of. "I'm here to sell my vacation."

"Take a number," came the reply.

"I need a number?"

"What do you think, you're the only one in Santa Fe who can't afford to go away on vacation?" the clerk looked at me shaking her head. "Take a number and get in line, right behind the mayor and the rest of the city councilors."

I should have known selling unused vacation to the city would be wildly popular. There was a little jostling in line and I looked up just as un-Mayor Larry was delivering a body check to Councilor Patty Bushee.

"Do you mind?" Bushee snapped.

"I'm sorry. I don't know what got into me. I guess I'm distraught over my cherry tree. It's dying because of the lack of water," un-Mayor said. He looked up and spied me. "You? What are you doing here?"

"Me?" I said. "I'm here to sell my vacation time or pay my water bill, whichever comes first."

"You don't work for the city," he said, narrowing his eyes. "Do you?"

"No, but why should you guys get all the breaks?"

"My poor cherry tree," the un-Mayor whined to no one in particular. "There's no water left to keep it alive."

"No water? Why don't we stop building all those subdivisions?" I

160

asked, noticing every one else moved a comfortable distance away from me.

"I've done everything for that tree. I've stopped showering," un-Mayor sniffed. "I brush my teeth only once a day. Angie and I drink bottled water at home."

"What about those subdivisions south of town?" I pressed.

"I remember when that tree was a mere sapling."

"Maybe we should stop extending the city limits," I said.

"My wife wanted me to plant a Russian olive," un-Mayor continued. "But I said to her, 'Honey, we can't eat those olives.' Ever since I was a young boy growing up in Santa Fe, playing hide 'n' seek in the Oldest House, I wanted a cherry tree."

"OK, let's say they can build, but they just can't hook up to city water. What about that?" I asked.

"Ever since I used to play pirates in the acequia, I dreamed of having a cherry tree."

"What about we let them build the houses, but we don't let anyone actually move in? That way you wouldn't lose votes or use water."

He turned to Patty Bushee. "How can I save my tree?"

"Don't ask me," she said. "I have a landscaping business. But there's no water so I'm not even working these days."

I Sure Don't

Oxymorons. I love 'em. Ever since I learned to spell the word. One of my Santa Fe favorites is the phrase, "I sure don't."

It's no secret that we do things a little differently here in the City Oh-So-Different. Let me give you an example.

My car was looking like one of those cars on which people write "Wash me" in the dust. So, instead of complaining about the weather, I drove into Squeaky Clean to get my car washed.

"I'll have to charge you extra because your car is dirty," the car wash attendant told me.

"Of course my car is dirty. That's why I'm here," I said right before I drove out.

John Gooch, who has been playing Happy Hour piano at the Eldorado Hotel for 16 years (times flies when you're having fun), called with this little Santa Fe story.

It seems Gooch was looking for a piece of furniture and called over to American Home.

"I'm looking for a tall, narrow, brass and glass shelving unit," Gooch told the clerk. (The man obviously has no taste.)

"Could you describe it for me?" came the reply.

And because Gooch has been in Santa Fe too long, he did.

You know you've been in Santa Fe too long when you have to drive 12 miles to the recycling place in town because the county allows us to recycle only brown glass.

You know you've been in Santa Fe too long when you go to bird stores for expensive bird seeds because the birds refuse to eat the cheap ones from Costco.

You know you've been in Santa Fe too long when you think it makes sense to pay more for free-range eggs because it costs the farmers more money not to house the chickens and to let them run free.

You know you've been in Santa Fe too long when the question paper or plastic (a no-win situation; just watch the clerk's face) is second only to red or green as the most important question you have to answer here.

You know you've been in Santa Fe too long when a typical Sunday outing is driving 10 miles to the county dump to recycle newspapers and cardboard, and stopping along the side of the road for a picnic.

You know you've been in Santa Fe too long when you haven't figured out why few people bother to vote in school board elections, but everyone likes to complain about the sad state of our schools.

You know you've been in Santa Fe too long when you've designed a house out of recycled, flattened aluminum cans, but are still trying to figure out where the latillas go.

You know you've been in Santa Fe too long when you begin looking for ways to make money from your pets and settle on finding a way to make money from dog hair.

You know you've been in Santa Fe too long when you recycle compost into art project. And a collector from Texas buys it.

When El Nino Was a Bulto

Before summer rolls in and the tourists get under our skin by asking silly questions like, "Why can't I have a glass of water with my dinner?" it's time to ascertain whether we've been in Santa Fe too long.

You know you've been in Santa Fe too long when your dentist begins filling a tooth left over from a past life.

You know you've been in Santa Fe too long when you used to go shoe shopping in the median on Old Pecos Trail.

You know you've been in Santa Fe too long when you remember when everyone in the state received a tax refund just for living in New Mexico.

You know you've been in Santa Fe too long when you think the digital divide is somewhere on the other side of Grants.

You know you've been in Santa Fe too long when you remember when El Nino was a carved bulto instead of a weather condition.

You know you've been in Santa Fe too long when most of your friends are here because their cars broke down 10 years ago and they're still waiting for the parts.

You know you've been in Santa Fe too long when you remember stopping in the middle of the road to have a conversation with someone driving the other way and no one ever blew their horn.

You know you've been in Santa Fe too long when you remember when a restaurant served three different nationalities of food, depending on what time of the day it was.

You know you've been in Santa Fe too long when you keep track of the seasons by the type of dress the guy with the beard is wearing.

You know you've been in Santa Fe too long when you research the lost language of Central Asia by stopping by the Allsop's because the clerk has a Ph.D in ancient linguistics.

You know you've been in Santa Fe too long when you think the perfect hostess gift is a quart of bottled water.

You know you've lived in Santa Fe too long when you think spelt is the past tense of spell instead of a grain.

You know you've lived in Santa Fe too long when you begin gardening with plastic flowers.

You know you've been in Santa Fe too long when you ask your guests if they went to the bathroom before leaving home because you don't want them using your water supply.

You know you've been in Santa Fe too long when you think white bread is a delicacy because the store where you shop doesn't carry it.

You know you've been in Santa Fe too long when you need a new astrological chart because your Saturn return has come back to haunt you.

Naming Your Child 501(c) 3

Fall is my favorite season in Santa Fe. The air is so fresh and the colors so beautiful, it literally takes your breath away.

I got up before dawn the other day, so I could drive up to the aspens and watch the sunlight silently steal through the trees.

If you haven't planned your own drive up into the National Forest this year, don't wait any longer. Now's the time, especially since the recent rains have spawned new growth along the forest floor.

If you're not making the time to do this because you've already driven up to see the changing of the leaves during some past year, maybe you've just lived in Santa Fe too long.

You know you've lived in Santa Fe too long when someone mentions drag racing and you begin thinking about what to wear.

You know you've lived in Santa Fe too long when you ask for vinegar to go with your fish and chips and the waiter brings out a bottle of 18-year-old Balsamic.

You know you've lived in Santa Fe too long when you name your child 501(c)3, because the initials mean more to you than anything else you can think of.

You know you've lived in Santa Fe too long when you realize you've never received a W-3 tax form because you always end the year with a handful of 1099s from all of your 12 part-time jobs.

You know you've lived in Santa Fe too long when you begin carrying a Filofax with the Aztec calendar.

You know you've lived in Santa Fe too long when all of your best friends are named after native shrubs but their kids are named John, Susan and Bill.

You know you've been in Santa Fe too long if you can't pass a school bus without imagining yourself driving it after painting it a rainbow's worth of colors.

You know you've lived in Santa Fe too long when you remember that long before there was Whole Foods, there was a loosely formed co-op of people exchanging food in the parking lot down at the rail yard.

You know you've lived in Santa Fe too long when you remember when Tia Sophia's took personal checks, but didn't take credit cards.

You know you've lived in Santa Fe too long when you remember when parking in the city was free, and so were you.

You know you've been in Santa Fe too long when you've been wearing the same pair of winter boots for six years and consider yourself lucky to have them.

You know you've lived in Santa Fe too long when someone shows you a $100 bill and you didn't think they were being made anymore because it's been so long since you've actually seen any bill over $20.

All the Mud That's Fit to Track

Ten minutes after it began snowing, the Santa Fe County Commission amended a four-year-old freeze on new development in Eldorado.

Although a number of Eldorado residents opposed the lifting of the moratorium after remembering their landscape die during the drought last summer, the governing body passed it anyway. Makes you wonder who they're working for.

Frankly, I wasn't even surprised, or maybe it's just that I've just been living in Santa Fe too long.

You know you've been living in Santa Fe too long when you find yourself driving the wrong way down a one-way street instead of complaining about other people doing it.

You know you've been living in Santa Fe too long when you begin to salivate when you see the colors red and green.

You know you've been living in Santa Fe too long when you know you could be a vegetarian if it were not for the green chile cheeseburgers at the Bobcat Bite.

You know you've been in Santa Fe too long when you're not surprised by the vote-counting debacle in Florida, you just wonder what took them so long to catch up with New Mexico.

You know you've been living in Santa Fe too long when you're no longer surprised by the amount of mud one dog can track inside the house after the snow melts.

You know you've been living in Santa Fe too long when you're no longer surprised that yet another prisoner has escaped custody since in the last 500 years, the only prisoner who never escaped was Wen Ho Lee, but then he wasn't guilty anyway.

You know you've been living in Santa Fe too long when the word "Frito" pops into your mind when someone asks you to name your favorite pie.

You know you've been in Santa Fe too long when you're not surprised Burro Alley has been closed to traffic, but are waiting for the same logic to prevail on Plaza traffic.

You know you've been in Santa Fe too long when you say the words "Kaune's chicken" with as much reverence as "Mom's apple pie."

You know you've been living in Santa Fe too long when you get tired of your relatives back East saying, "I didn't know it snows there. I thought it was the desert."

You know you've been in Santa Fe too long when some of the same kids you used to cut classes with in high school are starting their own charter schools.

You know you've been living in Santa Fe too long when you know all of the wood and stone sellers on Peddler's Corner (Old Las Vegas

Highway and Old Pecos Trail) by name and where their secret stone yard is located.

You know you've been in Santa Fe too long when you've never seen the last act of any opera because you can't stay awake that late.

You know you've been in Santa Fe too long when you remember when all the pharmacies were home-owned and corporate America wasn't dictating whether or not we could buy birth control pills.

You know you've been living in Santa Fe too long when you can remember when it really was The City Different.

In Search of Santa Fe Style

There they were, like a springtime herd of something we were warned about in science class. Guerilla art.

The shoes had returned to the median on Old Pecos Trail. I smiled so wide, my lips cracked (the result of too many summers in the sun).

At first, there was a lone hiking shoe. I was speeding along in my car, but I think it's a size 10 with rubber bottoms, man-made uppers, with a suave touch of suede (the result of reading too many catalogue descriptions).

The next day, there were a pair of children's sandals (scuffed but still wearable) a gold-colored sling back, a well-worn pair of men's work boots, a couple of odd tennis shoes, an Arizona-style Birkenstock and the mate to yesterday's hiking shoe.

Later that day, I was talking to Chris at the Sav-on pharmacy, which is where I spend a lot of my free time since HMO insurance companies dole out only enough pills to carry us through for 30 days, when I overheard a woman talking about the shoes on Old Pecos Trail.

When she asked the inevitable question of why they were there, I knew she was a newcomer. Had she lived here for a number of years, she would have known the answer: Because they are.

And if that doesn't sound like an answer your mother would give you, all I can say is that you must be living in Santa Fe too long.

You know you've been living in Santa Fe too long when you're not sure about going to the opening of the Santa Fe Opera, but you were first in line at the re-opening of Furrs Cafeteria on Cordova.

You know you've been living in Santa Fe too long when you remember when Santa Fe style was no windows, a false ceiling and no closets.

You know you've been living in Santa Fe too long when you recognize a familiar dog by name riding in the backseat of a car but haven't a clue about who its owner is.

You know you've been living in Santa Fe too long when an entire trailer is the main room in your house because you've just "added on over the years."

You know you've been living in Santa Fe too long when you begin thinking of lowering the springs on your Subaru, removing the door handles, chucking the leather steering wheel for a chain link job and joining the Alameda Cruise on Friday night.

You know you've been living in Santa Fe too long when you realize there are no copies of "Trailer Life" at the magazine rack at the local market, but there are four separate publications about Range Rovers, including two featuring special off-road equipment.

You know you've been living in Santa Fe too long when you realize the phrase "fixer upper" doesn't appear in the classified ads any more.

You know you've been living in Santa Fe too long when half of your friends have left town and have moved back again and have the same telephone numbers they had before they left.

You know you've been living in Santa Fe too long when you remember when Downtown Subscription was really Downtown.

You know you've been living in Santa Fe too long when you remember when all the fresh fish served at restaurants came from Denver.